Hello, Cruel World

Hello, Cruel World

101 Alternatives to Suicide for Teens, Freaks, and Other Outlaws

KATE BORNSTEIN

foreword by Sara Quin

SEVEN STORIES PRESS

New York | Toronto | London | Melbourne

Copyright © 2006 by Kate Bornstein

A Seven Stories Press First Edition

Seven Stories Press
140 Watts Street
New York, NY 10013
www.sevenstories.com

In Canada: Publishers Group Canada, 250A Carlton Street, Toronto, ON M5A 2L1

In the UK: Turnaround Publisher Services Ltd., Unit 3, Olympia Trading Estate, Coburg Road, Wood Green, London N22 6TZ

In Australia: Palgrave Macmillan, 627 Chapel Street, South Yarra VIC 3141

Library of Congress Cataloging-in-Publication Data
Bornstein, Kate, 1948-
  Hello, cruel world : 101 alternatives to suicide for teens, freaks, and other outlaws / by Kate Bornstein.
     p. cm.
  Includes indexes.
  ISBN-13: 978-1-58322-720-6 (pbk. : alk. paper)
  ISBN-10: 1-58322-720-2 (pbk. : alk. paper)
  1. Teenagers—Suicidal behavior—Prevention. 2. Adolescent psychology. 3. Self-help techniques for teenagers. 4. Sexual minorities—Psychology. 5. Minority teenagers—Psychology. I. Title.
HV6546.B67 2006
616.85'844505—dc22
2006004973

College professors may order examination copies of Seven Stories Press titles for a free six-month trial period. To order, visit www.sevenstories.com/textbook or send a fax on school letterhead to (212) 226-1411.

Book design by Jon Gilbert

Printed in the USA.

9 8 7 6 5 4 3 2 1

For my daughter, Jessica, and her children.
Just in case any of you need this one day.

For my mom, Mildred Vandam Bornstein, who
passed out of this world eleven years ago.
Mom, you should now be approaching the age that
you might want to read and use this book.

For all outsiders, freaks, misfits, nerds, geeks,
queers, and outlaws.
Please stay alive. We need you in this world
to keep things interesting.

In loving memory of Jake Barker (1980–2002).
Honey, I'm so sorry I didn't get this to you in time.
Wherever you are these days, I hope you and life are
on much better terms.

Acknowledgments

The longer you manage to live, the more people there are who have contributed to the quality of your life. In order to make more space for the actual book, I've had to limit these acknowledgments to those people who've most directly influenced this book.

To Barbara Carrellas, my partner in life, love, and art. Thank you for balancing my study of gender with your study of sex; my love of sadomasochism with your love of tantra; and my love of pussy with your love of pug.

Thanks go to friends, family, extended family, and early readers: Caitlin Sullivan, Kaylynn Raschke, John Emigh, David Harrison, Ava Apple, Jack Barker, Ann Pancake, Alan Bornstein, Roz Kaveney, Mary Dorman, Amy Scholder, Veronica Vera, Tony Phillips, Marsha Botzer, T. Cooper, Aidan Key, Holly Hughes, Esther Newton, Gail and Betsey Leondar-Wright, Troy Dwyer, Gail Harris, Gayle Landers, and Marsian De Lellis.

You're able to read this book thanks to the courage, persistence, and dedication of my editor at Seven Stories Press, Crystal Yakacki; my publisher, Dan Simon; and my literary agent, Malaga Baldi. Thank you all for believing in this project. Thanks, too, to my trusty ward and sidekick, Erin Markey, for keeping me organized. Thank you to Jon Gilbert and Phoebe Hwang for translating my rough layout sketches into something truly beautiful and functional.

I wrote a lot of this book in the woods of eastern Long Island in the sweet home of Lynn Birks and Judith Wit. I wrote the bulk of the 101 Alternatives in two Hell's Kitchen Starbucks, where the baristas made me feel right at home and where T-Mobile kept me connected to the Web. I wrote on a succession of Apple PowerBooks, using OS X. I used OmniOutliner Pro for my notes and outlines, and Microsoft Word for the actual writing as well as for the rough layout and early design of the book. I'm grateful to Scott Kelby for his workshops, tips, and how-to books that taught me how to do diddle all the images in this book in Adobe Photoshop. I'm also grateful to Dover Publications for their permission to use their images. And to Ron and Joe of Art Parts for their generous permission to use over twenty of their images. Thank you also to Snaggy and Nitrozac of geekculture.com for the lovely geek toon, and to Diane DiMassa for the use of her Hothead Paisan art.

There were times during the writing of this book when I found myself deep in despair. That's when I watched all seven seasons of *Buffy, The Vampire Slayer* (twice), and all the episodes of *Firefly* (three times, once with the commentaries turned on). So, thanks to Joss Whedon and to the casts and crews of those TV shows. I also re-read the ten volumes of my favorite graphic novel: *The Sandman*, by Neil Gaiman. And I kept my spirits up with the awesome Jamaican cooking of renowned neighborhood chef, Colin Drysdale.

I'm deeply grateful to Julia Ritchie, my life coach and therapist, for the insights she has given me. Thank you, Dr. Rona Vail at the Callen-Lorde Clinic in New York for my good health, and thank you Judy Reilly for untangling my financial records so I could go on writing. Thank you, dear Edward Maloney for a decade of really great hair. And thank you Dona Ann McAdams for making me look so good in all the photos you've taken of me over the past twenty years, especially my author photo for this book.

Thanks to Craig Dean, Ellie Deegan, Katya Min, and Felicia Gustin, who book my speaking and performance gigs. I've received encouragement and support from literally thousands of students, faculty, staff, and administrators in over one hundred colleges, universities, conferences, and high schools where I've had the honor and great pleasure to speak and perform.

Gone from this world are sweet Goose, the pug, as is my beloved cranky old Gwydyn, whose ashes now rest on the floor of the Ngorongoro Crater where he can chase zebras to his heart's delight. It's taken two pugs, two cats, two turtles, and a well-populated ant farm to make up the loss of you, pal.

Contents

Foreword

My grandmother was rumored to have told my mother that, if she let us continue to pick out our own clothes (brown snow-suits) and cut our own hair (mullets) and pierce our ears (only the right ear), my sister Tegan and I would turn into "lesbians." She was right, sort of.

I don't think it was my mother's support of our color-blind preferences in outerwear or the androgynous haircuts in elementary school that turned us into lesbians. But her patient, supportive parenting did leave me feeling fairly confident upon my arrival at the threshold of adolescence. Having outgrown our childhood nicknames for one another ("Brother"), Tegan and I transitioned somewhat successfully into junior high and a world of shoplifting, hand jobs, and drive-bys.

Still, junior high was hell on earth for me. Instead of fighting my way to the top echelons of popularity, I was happy playing make-believe games like "Jail" and "Orphanage" in the basement with my best friend. I was totally unprepared to face the emotional cannibalism of my bullies. At the insecure and irrational age of fourteen, turning to the administration of my school for any sort of help or support would have seemed a ridiculous and potentially dangerous effort. Forced to take refuge in many bathroom stalls, I planned my sick days months in advance.

It was at this point in my life that I realized almost everyone I knew was suffering. Terrible stories of sexual abuse, assault, and neglect by parents, teachers, and the system were so common I lost track of what had happened to whom. No adult or authority figure was prepared to take responsibility for the kids who challenged the system in any way. In the low-income neighborhoods where I grew up, out of control teen gangs were allowed and almost encouraged to run wild. Rather than looking at the symptoms and addressing the problems, the administration expelled these struggles right out into the street. It seemed like no one was even paying attention. I had friends who successfully made it to the tenth grade without ever learning how to read!

I know that the struggles I had in my teen years pale in comparison to some. Most of my friends made it out with scratches and bruises. But since then I have seen too many of those survivors fast-track it to jail, poverty, and drug addiction. What didn't get them in high school seemed to catch up to them later on in life. A narrow escape does not atone for a missing foundation of positive self-esteem and coping skills. What Kate Bornstein calls "Bully Culture" extends far beyond the halls of junior high: the struggle of youth as a social outlaw is the struggle of a lifetime.

What I deeply respect about *Hello, Cruel World* is that by standing shoulder to shoulder with marginalized and oppressed teens, Kate looks straight into the eyes of the bullies who seem to outnumber us and shows us how to successfully take a stand against them. Instead of a text heavy on statistics and psychological jargon, Kate bravely uses humor to collapse the wall of isolation and shame that is often associated with suicide (and with being a teenager). I take strength from this confident, honest book and from Kate's success as a compassionate human being who has courageously spoken out for all of us living outside of the box. We are being offered alternatives and insight from an ally who has been there and survived. This "verbal eye contact" is revolutionary and can be life-changing. Meet Kate's kind, steady gaze in this book: it is a sure-fire alternative to suicide, and I hope anyone in trouble will give it a try.

—Sara Quin
of Tegan and Sara
March 2006

Introduction

Hi, I'm Kate Bornstein.

I'm nearly sixty years old, and a lot of people think I'm a freak for a lot of reasons. I wrote this book to help you stay alive because I think the world needs more kind people in it, no matter who or what they are, or do. The world is healthier because of its outsiders and outlaws and freaks and queers and sinners. I fall neatly into all of those categories, so it's no big deal to me if you do or don't.

This is not a book of reasons not to kill yourself. No matter how many I could come up with, you'll come up with more reasons to go through with it. This is a book about things to do *instead*.

I've had a lot of reasons to kill myself, and a lot of time to do it in, and I have stayed alive by doing a lot of things that are considered immoral or illegal. I'm glad I did them all because I've really enjoyed writing this book. This may be a scary time for you, and if that's so, I hope that I can help you find your courage again. If we meet some day, let me know what worked.

PART 1

Hello, Cruel Me

Today could be the last day of your life. Whether or not you're thinking of killing yourself, you could die at any moment.

Still here?

Excellent! That's called staying alive.

Considering that these could very well be the last few moments of your life, why are you spending such precious time reading this book?

 And just who am I, trying to creep inside your head and talk to you about staying alive? You have every right to know more about me. So, here's me coming out to you: My name is Kate Bornstein, and I'm a transsexual.

Still here?

Excellent! That's called being interested in life's possibilities.

I'm not exactly a transsexual. A transsexual is a man who becomes a woman, or a woman who becomes a man, and I'm not a man, and I'm not a woman. I break too many rules of both those genders to be one or the other. I transgress gender. You could call me transgressively gendered. You could call me transgender. Me, I call myself a traveler.

I'm traveling through all sorts of identities, picking and choosing what works and leaving the rest behind. I shift and change in order to make staying alive more worthwhile. I shift and change in order to keep myself from getting stuck someplace where I'd rather be dead, or might as well be.

Sometimes I'm aware of shifting my identity, and other times I shift identities without even thinking about it, like a chameleon skillfully morphing its colors and markings to accommodate an ever-changing environment. They're not multiple personalities, they're all different ways of expressing me in the world.

Are you exactly the same person today that you were seven years ago? That day could have been the last day of your life, but it wasn't. Does it seem to you that you're different than you were then? In point of fact, you are a *completely* different person at this moment than you were even when you began reading this book. On a submolecular level, nothing about your body is in the same place as it was just a few moments ago. And then there's your heightened awareness that you really could be dead at any moment. So, are you the same person? I'm not saying you're not. I'm just asking: do you ever consider what it is that makes you the same person now as you were ten minutes ago, when so much of you is truly different?

Still here? Are you sure? Just kidding. That's called coming to terms with life through a synthesis of postmodern theory and Zen Buddhism.

I was a boy who didn't want to be a boy, and in the either/or, gotta-be-one-thing-or-another modernist world of the 1950s, the only alternative to boy was girl, which I wasn't allowed to be. No one talked about the possibility of being neither. So I worked real hard at being a boy. It was something I was conscious of doing all the time. I watched other boys and did what they did. I did what all the ads and movies and school text-books told me that boys do.

I watched for what to do right. I needed other people to validate my effort to be real. It was important that they saw me as one of them. I don't think I ever pulled it off. Their kind of realness seemed always to be out of reach. These days, I'm trying less and less to be a real *anything* but the real me, whatever that ends up being.

Have you ever pretended to be another kind of person so that someone would like you better, or maybe so they wouldn't hurt you? Have you ever changed the kind of person you were in order to make people believe you were somehow more real? How did you ensure that you were looking and behaving within acceptable social parameters?

Everyone consciously or unconsciously changes who they are in response to their environment or to some relationship that they are negotiating at any given moment. Every life form does that. It's a kind of phenotypic plasticity, an observable biological theory that says more or less that all life forms evolve according to their surroundings. They shift and change what they are so that their identity doesn't wind up causing their death and/or eventual extinction as a species.

Elephants stomping around in the polar regions of our planet evolved into woolly mammoths in response to the bone-deep cold. Their tropical ancestors in Africa and India retained their sun-resistant easier-to-cool nearly hairless gray hides. Life forms evolve not only over thousands of years, but sometimes over the course of just one lifetime. Some life forms can evolve in a little over a few minutes. Humans do that. Our spirits and brains seem to have the kind of genetic RAM and processing speed that it takes to shift identities on the spot, the way a chameleon shifts color.

Sometimes we use costumes to change who we are, sometimes we use drugs and alcohol. We admire people who can shift identities well and seemingly with few or no props: Robin Williams, Carol Burnett, John Belushi. They shuffle identities as effortlessly as a good poker player shuffles a deck of cards.

We don't learn to shift identities for purely whimsical reasons, or because we're bored or want to entertain people. It's something we do in order to survive. The ability to control who and what we are or seem to be in the world is a life skill we learn through practice, just like any other life skill. Have you been practicing?

The less consciously we evolve our identities—who we are and how we're seen in the world—the better the chances are that one day we're going to wake up and not know where we are or how we got there. The skills that used to work for us will have stopped working. Our identities always stop working for us at some point. Why? Because the world around us is moving forward in time. Standards of cultural identities change depending on generation, degree of multiculturalism, and who's sitting in the White House. Identities in culture

behave like software in an operating system: you have to keep an eye on what version you're using, and update it regularly, or you'll crash badly.

People who are reactionary try to keep the world from changing, rather than do the hard, but ultimately more realistic, work of changing themselves. People who don't see any way of changing themselves or the world spend a lot of time wishing they were dead.

When we consciously evolve toward an identity that we can live with, life becomes more of a game or a sport, like surfing. I'm not saying it's an easy or fun thing to do, just that it takes skill, it's exciting, and it's absolutely worth the commitment and sacrifice.

Growing up, I got pretty good at being boy. But boy wasn't an identity I could live with. Boy wasn't how I wanted to be treated, and boy was never how I wanted to act. Boy never allowed me to truly express myself. Every waking moment that I walked through the world as boy and man made me feel like a liar and a phony. But after I went through with my gender change, I found myself still living a life of working hard at being, only now I was working hard at being *girl*. Nothing in the paradigm of my life allowed for being neither. And the more I tried to be boy or girl, the less I seemed to measure up to *either*, and the less I wanted to stay alive. It finally got to the point where it just didn't seem worth it any more. It came down to this: should I kill myself or should I make myself a life worth living? And it wasn't so much the question that kept me alive or even my answer. What kept me alive was the notion that it was me who was asking the question.

Somewhere inside me there was a me that wanted to stay alive, whether I knew that me yet or not. The possibility of that began to tip the scales toward life. And then there was the fact that it was me and only me who could actually answer the question of to be or not to be. I took that to mean that if life had endowed me with the responsibility of wrestling with a question like that, then it stood to reason that it had also given me some means by which I could choose life over death with a minimum of suffering. Somewhere inside me there was an identity I could live with that would allow me to be both girl and boy—and neither to boot. The me I'm being today is the result of that reasoning, and I'm having a pretty good life. But that's my life. Your life is a different story.

Try this: Imagine the world as a place where anyone can safely and even joyfully express themselves the way they've always wanted to. Nothing about the bodies they were born with or what they choose to do with those bodies—how they dress them, or decorate, or trim, or augment them—would get people laughed at, or targeted, or in any way deprived of their rights. Can you imagine a world like that?

Stay with that image for a moment and envision yourself as the kind of person who lives happily and contentedly in that world. What gives you pleasure? What are the components of your iden-

tity that allow for that pleasure? How many components of that envisioned identity can you put in place in your *real* life in order to achieve real pleasure?

Envisioning the achievement of this kind of pleasure means that we need to talk about and deal with that which enables it: our desire and our sexuality. Sexuality is more than who we're attracted to. It is more than what we like to do in bed. It is a social identity. It is the way we experience the world around us in a positive, life-affirming way.

Think about someone you're attracted to—a movie star, or real person, or someone out of a comic or game. Anyone. Even someone you're not supposed to be attracted to but are. Just imagine that the two of you like each other in a really nice sort of way, and it makes you smile just to be sitting next to that person.

Now, how do you feel compared to how you felt just a moment ago, before you thought of the object of your affection? That's how thinking about—and coming to terms with—sexuality can help you want to go on living.

Try this advanced mode of the exercise you just did: Imagine sweet sex with a really great person or persons, and it's making both or all of you feel great. Go on, think of the best sex you've ever thought of, even if you've never had that kind of sex. Think about every kind of sex you can think of, especially if you're a virgin in any kind of sex and even if some people say it's not right for you to think about it.

Can you imagine being the kind of person who has that kind of sweet sex and relationship? If you can imagine it, you are completely capable of taking steps to realize it. It's a matter of trusting someone enough to let them know who you really are. Trust yourself first. You've managed to stay alive for the last few pages of some pretty heavy stuff. You've trusted me to more or less make sense of choosing life over death. That's how you trust other people. Just like that. Trust them to help you explore and understand your desire and sexuality.

I've long wanted to give my sexuality a name so that I could better understand it, and share it with other people. I tried to call myself a lesbian. I love women. I always have. All the big loves of my life have been women, including the three I've loved deeply enough to call my wife. I've wed three women, but I'm not a lesbian. I would have sex with Christian Slater, Johnny Depp, or David Duchovny in a New York minute. I just don't want a romantic relationship with any of them. Well, maybe Johnny Depp. Does that make me bisexual? No, because the textbooks tell me that bisexuals are men or women who love men and women, and that gets me back to not being a man or a woman.

If you were in this picture, who would you be?

I've tried to explain my sexuality using the words *sadomasochistic femme bottom*. Whoa! This is really easy to explain without having to warn you about sexually explicit material coming up. *Sadomasochistic* means that pain is something I can play with erotically, and that I enjoy playing safely, sanely, and consensually with other people who like to play with pain erotically. *Femme* means I like being girly, I like making butch women smile, and it makes me happy when someone thinks I'm cute. And *bottom* means that I like to be the one who's taking the pain, not the one who gives it. I've been an owned and collared slave, but I've also been a not-so-successful professional dominatrix. Still, how can I really be a sadomasochist when I enjoy plain old sweat-a-lot, laugh-a-lot, scream-a-lot vanilla sex so much? Like everything else, understanding my sexuality is a matter of having an appreciation for the ways in which my desire and pleasure changes.

Right now, I'm having the time of my life being a tranny dyke. Goodness, do you think I planned on that?

We all want an identity that makes life worth living. The good news is, you get to decide what pleases you and makes you feel the most secure. You get to decide which identity you are going to be or not be. It is up to you to travel bravely through the nature of your own desire to a place where you can take it or leave it. That's a sweet place to be. You can explore the nature of your desire through either sex or gender. How about a gender identity that's celibate, or that has sex with itself? Or sex with some deity? Have you explored all the possibilities?

So . . . how would you name your sexuality? Are you gay or lesbian? Are you heterosexual or bisexual? Are you monogamous? Polyamorous? Sex positive? Something else entirely? How many ways of being have you allowed yourself? Look, you're not even the same person you were ten minutes ago. None of us is. Are you straight? Only and forever? Are you queer? Only and forever? We change our attitudes, our opinions, and our relationships. We change our minds, our politics, our moods, our sympathies and our clothing. We simply change.

The Serenity Prayer is all about change. We ask for the serenity to accept the things we cannot change, the courage to change the things we can, and the wisdom to know the difference. My third wife, Jackie, taught me that one, bless her.

So, here, during what might be the last few moments of our lives, what do we know about each other, you and me? The best *I* can say is: Hello. I'm Kate Bornstein. I'm traveling.

And I can tell you this with certainty: You are worthy and capable of finding a way to live your life just the way you really are. And there are plenty of good people in the world who believe that a life like yours needs to be lived. If you work at being as fully you as you can possibly be, you will feel better.

And keep in mind that the you that makes life worth living today probably won't be the same you that makes life worth living this time next year. Identities aren't meant to be permanent. They're like cars: they take us from one place to another. We work, travel, and seek adventure in them until they break down beyond repair. At that point, living well means finding a new model that better suits us for a new moment.

I believe in the truth of you and so do a lot of other people, people you may not even know yet. Whatever you're being right now, wherever you've been traveling, and whatever you might become tomorrow, I believe in you.

This book is a lot about learning how to give yourself permission to go on living even when it really hurts. Right now you might be glad I've given you permission. Eventually, you'll no longer need anyone's but your own. Permission to do what? Permission to take yet another stab at putting together the kind of identity that makes you feel that you're being true to yourself and that life is worth living. Go ahead, give yourself permission to become the kind of person you've always dreamed you could be.

Hello, Cruel Bullies

Bullies can make life miserable. And I'm not just talking about kids, because bullies don't stop being bullies once they've grown up, they just get more sophisticated. The very act of reading this book is brave and transgressive in part because most systems we've developed as a culture to classify ourselves—systems like sexuality, gender, race, class, and age—are not typically questioned all that much. Those in political power these days actively discourage questions that challenge their bully culture. But  they don't hesitate to ask some pretty scary questions of their own about who we are as citizens of the world at the start of the twenty-first century.

Are you a terrorist, or aren't you?
Do you support terrorist activities,
or don't you?

And the most deeply probing
question of our time:

Are you with us, or against us?

If trying to answer these questions makes you feel at all uncomfortable, you're in good company. These questions are *designed*
to make you feel uncomfortable. They are designed to make you
not want to be the complex person that you are. Either/or questions are, for the most part, asked by bullies or by those who've
been beaten down by bullies and have joined their ranks.

That's why George W. Bush continues to ask the question, "Are
you with us or against us?" The United States has become a real
bully in the world, and Bush is the archetypal American bully
asking bully questions that aren't really questions at all.
Either/or questions—every single one of them—are another
way of saying, "It's my way or the highway."

Many either/or questions seem reasonable.

Are you drunk or sober?

Are you young or old?

Are you black or white?

Are you a man or a woman?

Are you happy or sad?

*Do you want to kill yourself
or keep yourself alive?*

One or the other. Simple. You don't need to think about it. You don't need to use your imagination, because the question itself dictates your only options.

In 1996, poet and activist Minnie Bruce Pratt addressed the Out-Write Conference of Lesbian, Gay, Bisexual and Transgender Writers with this chiding observation:

**"Our imaginations are in
thrall to the institutions
of oppression."**

WHAT'S IN A NAME?

I have this idea that naming ourselves beyond the either/or just might be the first step in freeing ourselves from the thralldom in which we're held by so many oppressive institutions.

I have this idea that those of us who question any aspect of our identities . . .

> those of us who are asking ourselves, "Who am I, really?"

> those of us who don't quite fit in, whether we can fool others about that or not . . .

I think we ought to be able to name ourselves, apart from the troublesome either/or language of the institutions that oppress us.

And I have this idea that whatever we name ourselves had better not play into the hands of those oppressive institutions, those institutions that insist we're this or that, one or the other, young or old, black or white, queer or straight, virgin or whore, hawk or dove, gendered or transgender.

I have this idea that every time we discover that the names we're being called are somehow keeping us less than free, we need to come up with new names for ourselves, and that the names we give ourselves must no longer reflect a fear of being labeled outsiders, must no longer bind us to a system that would rather see us dead.

Outsiders should call themselves outsiders, and we are mostly all outsiders
in this world, so we should welcome
one another's company.

Are you good or evil, male or female,
black or white, rich or poor? Are you
cool or are you a geek? Are you fat or
skinny? Are you a God-fearing Christian
or are you a servant of the Devil?

Can we begin to question the bully questions? Can we begin to question our slavery to an archaic, oppressive system? Can we call ourselves more than either/or?

If those of us who are still searching to discover who we are can't call ourselves more than either/or, who will?

If those of us who are struggling to discover the true nature of our love—and how we can freely express our love in the world—can't call ourselves more than either/or, who will?

And what about those of us who are still trying to figure out who we wanna be when we grow up? And those of us who are working to discover how we might fit into, and help heal, our world? If we don't call ourselves more than either/or, who will?

Neither/nor has become an increasingly present and visible identity in today's world. Those of us who are living it are faced with the life challenge of coming out of one closet or another and calling ourselves neither/nor whenever we safely can. Which is a hell of a lot easier said than done. Because of bullies, it's a lot easier to stay in a closet. It's a lot easier to shut ourselves down or eat a lot or eat nothing at all or cut on ourselves or take drugs. Because of bullies, we think about escaping or even getting even. Because of bullies—people who insist that we be one thing or another—their way or the highway—we think we might be better off dead.

It takes a great deal of work to discover a good reason to go on living within assigned identities that seem only to send us on a downward spiral towards death. One reason to go on living could certainly be to find out who *else* we might be, to free ourselves of identities we've been assigned by someone else—identities based on their standards, not our own. It is possible to break free of identities that are keeping you down. People who get stuck in underdog or outsider positions in life become great escape artists. That's me. I am positively slippery. How about you?

Most everyone defines most everyone else by their own standards, with little or no thought to the preferences and realities of the person they're defining. I do that. I call most all of us transgressively gendered. Everyone I've ever met either transgresses the rules of gender they've been brought up with, or they've at least had the impulse to do so. I'm not saying we're all cross-dressers or transsexuals or drag queens or drag kings or she-males or he/shes. I'm just saying that each of us tends to break some rule of gender. Are you defining someone else by your standards? Is someone doing that to you?

Here in the eye of America's über-culture, gender is chiefly used to signal our desire or power. So gender transgression is a red flag to bullies. Race, class, religion, and age are other signals of desire and power so they're also bully magnets, but gender is as good a place as any to examine how to deal with bullies. Look, do you mind that I'm talking so much about gender? It's what I know. It's something that you and I have in common: neither you nor I live up to being a perfect man or a perfect women. Right? Okay, with that in mind, let's take a look at . . .

A BRIEF HISTORY OF PEOPLE WHO HAVE BUCKED THE BULLY SYSTEM OF GENDER

Let's start with the early feminists of nineteenth-century America. The women who first said, "No!" The women who said, "My body and my mind don't belong to you, mister, or to anyone else." Those women said, "I won't be a woman the way you want me to be a woman." I have this idea that those women broke a lot of rules of gender in their day. Those feminists transgressed gender rules. They transgressed gender. They were transgender. People were mean to them because of that.

In the minds of the institutions that oppressed them, they were no longer real women. They needed to band themselves together under some flag, so they called themselves the Women's Movement.

Well, they weren't men, and it would have been terrifying to call themselves anything other than *women*. They were terrified to label themselves outsiders. But, in the simple act of calling them-

selves women, they named themselves after the system that had oppressed them for so long. It seems, in Minnie Bruce Pratt's words, that

their imaginations were in thrall to the institutions that oppressed them.

The next chapter of gender activism was written by the early gay rights activists. They tackled the law of gender that says loud and clear, "Real men love women, real women love men." "No we don't!" cried the homosexuals.

And these pioneers transgressed a deeply rooted rule of gender. Lesbians and gays transgressed gender. Lesbians and gays are transgender. And they needed to band themselves together under some flag.

But it's a terrifying thing to say, "Hey, I'm a man who loves men, so maybe I'm not a real man!"

And it's a terrifying thing to say, "I'm a woman who loves women, and so what if I'm not a real woman!"

People were even meaner about that kind of talk back in the late nineteenth and twentieth centuries than they are today. It was difficult enough to say the lesbian and gay stuff, and in most areas of the world, it still is. No one was ready to hear not-man, not-woman. So they called themselves lesbian *women* and gay *men*, and they said things like, "We're just like you."

They named themselves after the system that had oppressed them for such a long time. By the simple act of naming themselves women and men, it seems, in Minnie Bruce Pratt's words, that

> *their imaginations were in thrall to the*
> *institutions that oppressed them.*

Next up on the march of gender liberation was the Bisexual Movement, and these folks really shook things up. These bisexual folks came along and said:

Gender's got nothing to do with romance.

Gender's got nothing to do with sexual preference.

Gender's got nothing to do with love.

That shook *everyone* up, you betcha.

But they needed to band themselves together under some flag, and since it was terrifying enough to say that their love is mutable, they called themselves bisexual *women* and bisexual *men*. They named themselves after the system that had oppressed them for such a long time. By the simple act of naming themselves bisexual men and women, it seems, in Minnie Bruce Pratt's words, that

> ***their imaginations were in thrall to the institutions that oppressed them.***

And that brings us closer to present-day gender transgressive politics. Nowadays we've got transsexuals on the scene. Transsexuals and transvestites and two-spirits and intersex and drag kings and drag queens and he/shes and cross-dressers and lions and tigers and bears, oh my! And we're saying gender isn't rigid—it's fluid. We're saying gender isn't permanent—it's mutable. You can fuck with it. You can queer it up real good.

 But sure enough, we're about to do the same damned thing. We're calling ourselves female-to-male and male-to-female. We're *male* cross-dressers, or *female* impersonators.

We needed to band ourselves together under some flag, and we have been too terrified to call ourselves anything other than some sort of man or woman.

And by the simple act of calling ourselves some sort of man or woman, it seems, in Minnie Bruce Pratt's words, that

> *our imaginations are in thrall to the institutions that oppress us.*

We need to free our imaginations. We need to free ourselves from any system that would oppress us, even the ones that most people believe are "natural."

I have been looking for nearly three decades to find something in the world that's a natural either/or, and I haven't found a damned thing that doesn't have *some* shade of gray.

After considering the black-and-white assumptions we make about gender, I've had to question the importance of being *any* kind of man or woman.

Now here's the hard part, the part that's going to sound like I'm contradicting myself, but please bear with me. It's what I do.

Most of us in the world are men or women. I mean, duh! At least that's what we are in the eyes of the law. When the bullies come after us, they're going to separate us into men and women, and that's what we'll be in the eyes of the people carrying the guns and the billy sticks. No matter what we claim ourselves to be, we get herded into one place or another: the boys' locker room or the girls' locker room, the ladies' room or the gentlemen's room, the men's prison or the women's prison. No matter which side wins the "war on terror," gender outlaws will remain outsiders.

And what's that got to do with you? Well, most everyone who steps outside an either/or cultural law will become and remain an outsider or an underdog. Are you breaking some either/or cultural law, just by being who you are? If so, you're not alone. All the world's great civil rights movements have sought to harmlessly break some cultural bully standard. And all the outlaws who survived those civil rights movements have learned an important lesson. We understand that we can be outsiders and be miserable about it, or we can be outsiders and enjoy the fuck out of ourselves until we're old and weird and happy just being our geeky, freaky, outlaw selves. Understanding *that* is how we stay alive in a world that doesn't like who or what we are, what we look like, who we love, or how we act.

The eyes of those who would make us one or the other don't have to be *our* eyes. You don't have to look at the world the way you're told to look at the world. People who refuse to see beyond freak or geek or queer or bitch or nigger or kike or Muslim or fat or poor or crippled are wrong to do that. You don't have to look at yourself with their eyes. Ever.

Their voices don't need to be *our* voices. If someone is telling a lie, whether it's about you or anything else, you've got every right to call it a lie. You don't have to believe in or repeat any lies that you've been told. And just because the president of the United States mispronounces *nuclear*, it doesn't mean *you* have to. Claiming your own voice and language can be your best line of defense against any bully culture and any government that practices a politic of domination and exclusion. You are entitled to live bully-free and in a healthier political climate than that. It's possible.

Those of us who insist we're neither/nor are the oddballs and the outsiders in an either/or world. We have our individual outsider struggles. We fight our own unique fights, maintain our own unique cultures, all the while knowing we're fighting side by side with other outsiders, underdogs, and outcasts, all of us together. How about you?

What either/or standard are you refusing to buy into? Is there some my-way-or-the-highway choice you're having difficulty reconciling with your health or happiness? How can you rid yourself of an identity assigned to you by someone who's got the power to enforce the assignment?

How did those of us who want to be more than either/or end up with the short end of the stick when it comes to the free expression of our harmless desires? And how can we find some common ground . . . even among ourselves?

I think we can start simply and effectively by following the path laid out by the founders of the United States of America when they created this country in response to what they perceived to be intolerable cruelty and oppression. They were seeking their right to life, liberty, and the pursuit of happiness.

GIVE ME LIBERTY, OR GIVE ME DEATH

I'm going to open this next section by quoting the Declaration of Independence of the United States of America. I'll close by quoting the King James edition of the Bible. I figure that between the Declaration of Independence, the Bible, and our hearts—yours and mine—we ought to find some common ground.

Now, it would seem at first glance that life and liberty are a lot more important than happiness, especially after the terrorist attacks on the United States and the terrifying government that has established itself here in the name of national defense. But in my understanding of life, the highest quality of life, the entire purpose of liberty and perhaps what each and every human being on the planet has in common, is indeed the pursuit of happiness. So, it's happiness I'm going to talk about.

Two hundred years after the founding of this country, why are those of us who don't fit into some either/or told that our pursuit of happiness doesn't count? Are we going to continue nit-picking over exactly which happiness is legal and important, and which happiness is illegal and unimportant? Who has the right to say whose happiness is right? It all comes down to the mythology we grew up with.

Some of us have never felt included or welcome in whatever system of belief was bullying us, even the one that we were a part of. Some of us were forced to seek out mythologies that sang to us from the popular culture in the voices of movie stars or television characters. We have looked for myths that include us in great novels, music, the latest comic book, or even some stupid advertising campaign. We'll look *anywhere* for a mythology that embraces people like ourselves.

But even with our wildly different mythologies, one thing most of us can agree on is that we'd like to make some wild, glorious, mind-blowing love with someone who is our dream-come-true lover or lovers. Can't we agree on that? We want a little romance. We want to walk through the park on a spring day, holding hands. Most all of us would like something along those lines.

Well, that's one area of happiness all of us, all the wildly different outsiders we are, can start to agree on then, isn't it? We can agree on that. Okay, so then when did we stop agreeing to simply have a lovely day? When did we first run into a social institution that oppressed us?

I'd say it was back in junior high school, and I'd say we need to inspect more closely the time when most of us first stopped ourselves from pursuing happiness as we had once defined it.

I wanna do a little check-in here. Did you think that junior high was absolutely the best time of your life? Ask around. Not too many people feel that way.

When it comes to making sense of our lives and finding a reason behind living or dying, there's no end to the things we can choose to believe in. On this continent alone, some of us grew up Christian, some of us Jewish, and some Unitarian. Some of us were raised Buddhist, some Quaker, or Muslim, Hindu, or Wiccan. Some of us were even raised Scientologist. Many of us have been taught that our own mythology is the right, or only, one. This makes coexistence way tougher than it needs to be. Mythologies with more power than others to enforce their beliefs bully the world and make it difficult, or nearly impossible, to live differently from their traditions and from their ideas of purity and righteousness. Ideally, nobody would wanna impose their beliefs on anyone—we would just try to prevent meanness and preserve everyone's right to pursue happiness.

If you were in this picture, who would you be? No biggie, I'm just curious.

Who makes up the student population of junior high school? Kids whose hormones are raging and whose bodies are changing, and that's signaling that they're becoming men and women. But the culture says *that* won't happen for another decade or so, so they're not yet men and women, but they're too old to be called *kids*. In this way, youth itself is a type of neither/nor, and therefore outlaw, identity.

We throw all these no-longer-children, but not-yet-men and not-yet- women, into a social situation with each other where they're supposed to learn things, but the things they *want* to learn are:

How can I be popular?

What do I do about the crush I've got on her?

What can I do about the strange way he makes me feel attractive?

How can I keep myself from getting laughed at?

Why can't I be more like them?

Why don't they like me?

Here's a factoid for you. I heard it on ABC's *Nightline*. It seems that each and every school day of the year an average of 166,000 children stay home from school to avoid being bullied. Ouch! And more and more kids are turning to violence on themselves or others. There are those class freaks who, after years of being bullied, ignored, left out, and humiliated, react vio-
lently and with the same mean spirit with which they've been treated. Outsiders fought back violently and inexcusably, for example, in Columbine High School and Thurston High School, the Pentagon and the World Trade Center. By leaving no options for an outsider in the world, a bully culture engineers its own destruction.

 So, how do we care for kids? *All* kids? How do we help them with what they really wanna learn? We don't. We tell them what time of day they need to be in a certain seat. We teach them about the world the textbook publishers would like us to believe we live in, with no mention of the kids who grew up and never fit

in. We give them strict either/or's to conform to, and punish them when they don't or can't. And when the door closes after they leave our classrooms, we hope to whatever god or goddess we believe in that they won't kill each other. Thankfully, most kids don't.

As kids, most of us didn't kill the class freaks.

But, we developed something equally effective:

We knew how to make the class freaks want to kill themselves.

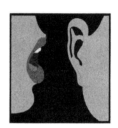

If the kids being picked on have the strength to withstand the stares, the laughter, the cruel pranks, the harassment, the beatings, or the rape, if those kids live, they very likely will learn how to make themselves invisible. Like the gay kid or lesbian kid, the stoner, the Muslim, or the radical lefty. Sometimes they can hide. Hiding successfully, covering up what could get you called freak, that's called passing. Maybe that's you?

And what about the kids who *can't* hide?

What about the boy who wears a prayer cap, or the girl who wears a religious head scarf to school? Or the kid whose family can't afford the latest fad in sneakers, or the only black or brown kid in class? What about the boy who wants to be Britney Spears, the girl who doesn't fit in the latest style of size two jeans, or the boy who starves himself so that he can? How about the too-tall or too-short kid, or the nerdy kid with geek glasses? Is there something about *you* that you can't hide?

What're we gonna do about all the kids that the culture labels oddballs? Because they're always gonna be there, pushing the borders of what's acceptable, pushing the culture to grow and test itself.

Remember the culture that all those hormonally crazed kids adopted? The one that says be like us, be just like us, or we'll drive you to suicide? Do we really think that's the best way to deal with people? Do we think that's a healthy social dynamic to foster? I'm going to guess you're saying, no, no . . . I don't want a world like that. If you've already managed to survive elementary school, junior high, and high school, I'm going to guess you're very glad you're out of there.

Well then, *so what* if a kid wants to learn Klingon as a third language? Who's to say that's not a cool thing to do? Damn, I own two *Star Trek* uniforms, and I make 'em look *good!*

And *so what* if a girl gets a crew cut and lets her chin hair grow? Who's to say that's not what she needs to do to survive in the world with some pride and integrity?

So what if a kid speaks with an accent, worships another God, and enjoys different kinds of music and food and dance? What happened to their right to pursue happiness?

Sure, we're different. Sure, some of us are weird and freaky. There are more and more visibly weird and freaky people in the world these days, and it's high time we stop carrying forward the junior high school dynamic of excluding them all from our lives or worse . . . nailing them to some cross.

I think it's brave of you to be sitting here, reading this book, even if you're reading for an extra credit assignment or because your therapist costs too much and someone talked you into trying this book. Hey, there are less terrifying ways to get extra credit and therapy. But why do you suppose that this is unusually brave of you unless we as a culture are still operating on the social dynamics we developed in junior high school?

That junior high dynamic is dependent in part on believing that outsiders, people like me, for example, are evil or godless, or that we're unpatriotic, or in need of a cure or salvation. Am I, do you think? Does someone think that way about you? That's called oppression.

One institution of oppression that each and every one of us can actively dismantle each and every day of our lives is the system we developed for *ourselves* back when we were no longer kids, but not yet men or women. The junior high dynamic may in fact be a cornerstone of *many* of the institutions that oppress us. So, how do we begin to dismantle it? The Bible says it better than I ever could:

When I was a child, I spake as a child. When I became an adult, I put away my childish things.

St. Paul, 1st Corinthians

Some high school students objected to my using a quote that lumped all childish ways into a category that must be done away with. To clarify things so that they work out nicely for everyone, I don't think we need to put aside *all* our childish ways . . .

just the mean ones. I think it's time for all of us to put away the childish things that don't work in the lives of kind, generous adults. I think we need to find alternatives to saying, or even thinking, childish things like, "Hey Faggot, Hey Cunt, Hey Nigger . . ." I think we need to find alternatives to saying, or even just thinking, childish things like, "You're too fat to be on our side," or too ugly, or too poor, or too Arab . . . I think we need to find alternatives to saying, or even just thinking, childish things like, "You're either with us, or you're against us . . ."

I think, instead, we should try something like this: "Excuse me . . . I hope I'm *not* interrupting," and only when we've determined that we're truly not interrupting someone or intruding on their privacy, do we proceed to ask, "I find you fascinating and so different from me. Might I ask you what your life's been like? I think we could learn something from each other."

How about *that* for putting aside childish ways that no longer work in the lives of kind, generous, inclusive adults? Isn't that easy?

We've been doing politics by exclusion in this country. Politics by us-versus-them. We do politics by exclusion in our schools and on our college and university campuses. We do politics by exclusion on a national and international level, and in corporate America.

Politics by exclusion may have had some value in the early days of our country, just like us-versus-them had some value in our childhoods—it gave us the illusion that we weren't outsiders, that we actually belonged to something. But the sense of belonging to something exclusive has got to change because we can no longer afford to keep people on the outside of things.

This growing-up nation we're part of is a whole lot bigger than it was a little over two hundred years ago, and part of the responsibility of being grown-up and bigger is giving a helping hand to all of those who still don't quite fit in, including those of us who don't fit in because our pursuit of happiness is two, or three, or seven bubbles left of center. I am saying that everyone would benefit from a change in the dynamic that oppresses us all in one way or

another. I am asking you to do something, anything, every day to change the way we as a culture have been dealing with difference.

Changing our cruel, childish dynamic is not anything that can be legislated. A new, inclusive, and compassionate politic must be lived by more and more people every day, free from the institutions that would enthrall them. It's got to start with each and every one of us. We need to include in our loving, caring, generous, and compassionate lives people who share our loving, caring, generous, and compassionate values, no matter their race or politics or religion, no matter their gender or sexuality. We need to work on behalf of *everyone* who's being oppressed by a system we bought into as children and never bothered to change.

Are you queer or straight?

Are you black or white?

Are you a man or a woman?

Look, I want to be a good and better person every day of my life. I want to be the best possible me I can be. I want to live in a world where people won't try to hurt me for trying to achieve happiness the best way I've found to do so. I assume that other people want that, too. You want to be a good and better person. I believe that. So, let's put aside the mean ways of doing things that we developed because, for some reason or other, we couldn't see that there were other options.

We can begin by celebrating difference. Let's stop hiding difference away where we don't have to look at it or think about it. Let's stop teasing, attacking, or bombing the hell out of difference just because it's not like us. Let's stop "tolerating" or "accepting" difference, as if we're so much better for not being different. Instead, let's *celebrate* difference, because in this world it takes a lot of guts to be different and to act differently. Exactly *how* we celebrate difference is for each of us to discover. But any political movement we support must be one that truly celebrates difference. *That's* how we start to put an end to the bully culture that's spreading across this country and the world at such an alarming rate.

Okay, now we've got some questions to raise. Are we men or women? Black or white, old or young, straight or queer, flag-waving patriots or traitors to our nation?

And who's been *insisting* that we be men or women, black or white, old or young, straight or queer, flag-waving patriots or traitors to our nation?

Can we implicate the people who are insisting we be either/or? Can we name some names? Can we get the truth out in the open? The truth about this social illness that starts as a way to cope in junior high, and turns into America's bully culture? More importantly, can we be more than the either/or the bullies want us to be? Can we be both/and?

Look, there is more and more rock-hard evidence to prove that any either/or system by which we attempt to categorize people is a product of our imaginations. There is more and more evidence to prove that binary systems of classification exist only in our minds.

Here's a good challenge for you: free your imagination from the institutions that enthrall you. And when you've finished doing that, go help some other people free theirs.

As outsiders in junior high, we never dreamed of questioning people who asked us are we one thing or another, are we with them or against them. But all that's changed now. You get to dream and live yourself a good life starting today.

Hello, Cruel Desire

What you desire exists just above or beyond you, and it always will. That's why it's called desire. Desire is yearning for something you don't have. Desire is wanting. What is it that *you* want?

Chasing your desire is like chasing perfection: you find joy in coming as close as you possibly can, and then you try all over again. If you're lucky, this delightfully insatiable chase ensures your quality of life until the day that you die.

Desire is drive and motion. It can bring urgency, spontaneity, and purpose to life. It is in making a move toward realizing something that you want—even and especially if it's not for yourself—that you give yourself a reason to go on living.

You get a taste of something you want, and you want more. There's nothing wrong with that. Hell, there's nothing better. Our desires are signposts to living a better life.

Desire can be for anything or anyone, or for nothing you can put a label on. Desire can be for sex. Have you ever had a sexual desire? Then you know what it means to want. So, what kind of sex do you want?

Well? Did you feel a change in your own energy when you came up with an answer to that question? Did anything tingle? That's called erotic energy. It's your body's way of telling you where to look for pleasure and fulfillment. Where do you want to focus all that great erotic energy that's been simmering inside you? Have you had a great orgasm recently? Ever? Have you helped someone else have a great orgasm recently? Ever?

Have you ever wanted the kind of sex that could get you in trouble?

How did your body respond when you answered *that* question? Sex gets everyone into trouble. Everyone. But that doesn't mean sex is a bad thing. A lot of very good people think with great longing about the kind of sex that could get them into a great deal of trouble. Desire—including, but not limited to, sexual desire—makes life less worth living when we become too attached to it, or when it is misused or abused, such as in the following cases:

Desire gets us into trouble *when we believe that having or not having something will make us a better or worse person.* That's just not true. You are a perfectly fine and whole person just the way you are. Being a better person depends on your intentions to ease suffering for yourself and others.

Desire gets us into trouble *when we've not yet spotted and named specifically what it is we really want.* So we end up wanting whatever someone else tells us we should want. There's a

proverb that's fitting here: if you don't stand for something, you'll fall for anything. I learned that one at a corporate seminar. More of the corporate world should keep that in mind, don't you think? Naming our desires isn't a one-time deal, though, because our desires are always changing through circumstance, taste, and the constant narrowing down of what it is we truly desire.

Desire gets us into trouble *when people who have more power than we do make us believe that wanting what we want is wrong, sick, bad, or evil.* Consequently, we come to believe that even if we don't actively pursue our desire, we are wrong, sick, bad, or evil just for *wanting* the object of our desire. Just not true. Unless what you want means being mean to someone else, there's *nothing* you could want that's wrong, sick, bad or evil. And if what you want involves being mean to yourself, well, then you've got a hard life ahead of you. You have some healing to do so that you can love and be kind to yourself. But you are not wrong or bad or evil.

Desire gets us into trouble *when we didn't, don't, can't, or won't get what we want and that leaves us feeling sad, angry, jealous, greedy, stingy, hopeless, scared, violent, abused, and/or abandoned.* Buddhists believe that desire is the cause of all suffering. Most of their religious teachings are all about how to end suffering for all sentient beings everywhere. Yes, there's a big difference between the suffering that comes from not having or losing a toy and the suffering that comes from not having or losing a parent or a friend. However, it is the case that any unfulfilled desire may bring a great deal of pain, sometimes enough pain to make you want to die. That kind of pain always passes. Always. It's not bottomless. It has an end. Everyone goes through a time in their life when all there is to living is staying alive one day at a time.

Desire gets us into trouble *when getting what we want depends on something bad happening to someone else.* I'm going to assume that you know well enough not to act on that kind of desire.

> Try this one: Make a list of what you want. Put a check mark next to the items on your list that could get you in trouble or have gotten you into trouble. For each of those items, see which of the above five factors apply.

I write postmodern sociopolitical theory about sex and gender. How about that? I never intended to devote my life to the deconstruction of binaries. Growing up, I just wanted to be pretty. That was my greatest, most mind-consuming desire. My want was always with me. I was a fat, awkward, nerdy teenage boy who wanted to be a thin, graceful, sexy teenage girl. Everything about wanting that made me a bad, sicko pervert. And as trivial as my desire might sound, the sheer impossibility of ever fulfilling my desire was enough to make me think about killing myself. The irony is that nothing about my desire was harmful to anyone else.

I was nearly forty years old when I finally realized that and began a long journey to change my identity. I started with my body. I lost weight. I worked out. I studied what it meant to be gracious and graceful, and I practiced that as best I could, given the body I've got. I read every feminist theory book I could get my hands on. I changed my physical body to female as far as I could. And finally, during the past ten years or so, I've been gradually giving myself permission to be sexy.

Let's take a look at your desires, why you've got them, and what to do about them when they are hurting you.

Being sexy and being ashamed of our sexual desires are not compatible feelings. When I finally began to look at sex from a female point of view, I had to deal with multiple layers of shame about my body, one at a time, until I eventually crossed a line where I was more tickled when I looked in the mirror than I was ashamed. My ability to enjoy life grew in direct proportion to my unwillingness to believe and obey cultural, religious, political, or legal restrictions to my harmless desires. I'm giving myself permission to feel sexy.

> *What makes you feel sexy?*

> *What would life be like if you felt more sexy than you feel right now?*

> *What did your body feel like when you answered these questions?*

Sex, gender, and desire are all things you can learn to manage in your life. Your life is worth living if for no other reason than to learn how to selflessly pursue your desires.

So . . . do you feel sexy?

Really, think about it. Do you?

Is feeling sexy important to you . . . or not? I'm saying either way is okay.

But when sexual desire is on an upswing in your life, there's value in knowing when it's a good time to express how sexy you feel. It's excellent to know and to be able to judge for yourself when expressing your sexy self might not be such a safe thing to do. It's something you must learn how to do in life—figure out how your desires fit in your day-to-day. I'm learning how to put sexy into everything I do . . . with respect for where I am, without scaring or intimidating whoever I'm with, because I want sexy to be fun. So, given the history of my life, what does that make me now?

Am I a man?

Am I a woman?

Am I a postmodern theorist?

Am I something to be studied in a clinic?

Am I something to be laughed at on the street?

All I've done all my life is ask the questions that have fried my brain. Asking these questions over and over again eventually helped me realize that no one could answer them but me. That little epiphany made it possible for me to give myself permission to walk in the world and express my values, for the most part, the way I like to express them.

I'm giving myself permission to feel sexy, and it's so much fun! I love walking down the streets of New York City these days. I'm smiling at people and people smile back. I've always wanted that. That's how I've wanted to walk in the world ever since I was a hippie boy who wanted to be a hippie girl. And I'm

The way I'm living right now is the closest I've ever gotten to the deities I finally found and managed to incorporate into my life: the movie stars. When I was a kid, that meant Audrey Hepburn in *Breakfast at Tiffany's* . . . she was for delight, and Liza Minnelli in *Cabaret* . . . she was for sexy. When I was a baby dyke, my total heroine was Linda Hamilton in *Terminator II*. I went blonde on account of Geena Davis in *The Long Kiss Goodnight*. These days, I've got Goddesses for all the ages I've ever been. My younger Goddesses include characters played by Angelina Jolie, Jewel Staite, and Alyson Hannigan. And I'm into anime like Sailor Moon, Ranma 1/2, and even Pokémon. I think love, sex and gender are like Pokémon, and I want to catch 'em all!

caring less and less what people think they see when they spot me. I used to scare people. I had a hell of a chip on my shoulder. But I don't get the jeers, not much anymore. I stop traffic now. Sometimes, a lot really, I get this stare that says, "Oh my God, what are you?"

But it's not a mean stare, it's not a stare of horror, because I know—I've come to believe—that what they're seeing when they see me is something cute. And when they stare at me and their eyes say, "Oh my God, what are you?" I smile at them, or sometimes I'll give 'em a wink. When they stare at me now, I say. "Hello, isn't it a beautiful day?"

And one by one, they blink, and smile, and say, "Yes. Yes, it is." It could be pouring rain outside. Doesn't matter. We've connected, and that makes it a beautiful day.

I love connecting with people, and since I'm not a man and I'm not a woman, I've had to find new ways to connect with people. I've been trying to connect with *you* through this book. And I've been connecting with the world by giving myself permission to be sexy, no matter what kind of abomination that makes me in the eyes of someone else's God. All my life, I've never had a God that loved me for all my weird, harmless eccentricities. How about you? If you indulged in all your fantasies, would God still love you? Is that a problem? Does that make life hard to manage? There are ways to deal with that.

There was no ready-made, off-the-rack religion that gave me a God to believe in, not a freak like me. I was born into Judaism, and according to its language of desire, I was an abomination. There were no answers in Judaism anyway, only questions. Their holiest book, the Talmud, places value on multiple inter-

pretations of a single concept. The more ways you could look at something, the wiser you would be.

Isn't that great? That's what I learned. That's how I look at life. That's how I look at my gender. That's how I look at my desire. I've been living through multiple interpretations of some basic me, identity after identity after identity. *I want to know what it's like to be what I'm attracted to.* With each successive incarnation, I get closer and closer. That's how I use my desire as a compass. I want to feel it in my body. That's become the nature of my desire. That's my understanding of what others must mean when they talk about the love of God. That's what makes me feel holy and in a state of grace.

When God says no to your harmless desires, it's time to find another God. The Gods and Goddesses who reflect your desire are out there, waiting for you to knock at their temple doors. Each of us—sex and gender outlaws and in-laws alike—must find our own spiritual path that lets us be sexy and have fun on our own terms. We have every right to search for Gods and Goddesses who live the way we ourselves would most love to live. You get to choose a more welcoming, supportive deity, theology, philosophy, belief system, hero/ine, friend, and/or role model. The greatest thing you can do for yourself is to discover an ethical, blissful way to go on living your life.

One cornerstone in my quest for a spiritually realized sexy life is the understanding that there will always be more ways to interpret my sexy, fluidly gendered self. How about you? How many ways can you safely be sexy? Or is that something you don't think about very much? Maybe being sexy is something you think about *too* much?

Nothing fuels desire more than its denial. Desires become all consuming to the degree that we don't explore them. The exploration of your desire does not mean you have to indulge in it right this minute or ever. You can read about what people have to say about your sexual desires. You can rent movies. You can play role-playing games online. You can go to a meeting of people who have desires similar to yours, or move to a town where they have things like that.

When desire becomes the leading edge of your life, if only for a brief moment, you have every right to explore it. And you have every right to keep yourself safe, healthy, and free. That means you have every right to say "NO" to your own or anyone else's desires that might endanger you or make you uncomfortable. You have every right to talk with someone you trust about what's going on, and if you have never done that, now would be a good time to start talking or at least start looking for someone to talk with. Exploring your desire all by yourself is brave but ultimately kind of dumb. Like when I tried climbing a mountain in Colorado. I'd never had a lesson. I was driving west, a nice Jewish boy like me. I got to the Rockies, and I pulled my car over and started climbing. Brave, but ultimately kind of dumb. I fell off the mountain, thirty feet down into a fluffy snowbank. Lucky me. Find someone to talk with about your desires before you jump into them.

A good starting place in the exploration of your sexual desire would be to determine the kind of person or people you're attracted to. Go on, give that one a few moments' reflection. What are some qualities, physical and otherwise, of the people you are attracted to? And now the surprise twist: what would it be like to be that kind of person yourself? I'm not talking about changing your body, although that's what I did to the extreme. Why did I do this? Well, some people describe the journey from one gender to another as the process by which people strive to make their bodies more congruent with the gender they perceive themselves to be. I agree with that one. That's what I've tried to do.

The problem was, I never really knew what gender I perceived myself to be. I knew what I *wasn't*. I've always known what I wasn't. I got messages from my family, from the magazines I read, the television I watched, from the schools I went to, the middle class I grew up in, and the white race I've always seemed in North America to be, even though the rest of the world would type my race as Jew. It all told me to be what I was not and what I could never want to be. Nobody knows the troubles I've seen!

Nobody knows the troubles I've seen, except everyone who's ever been made to think they're not a real man.

Nobody knows the troubles I've seen, except everyone who's ever been made to think they're not a real woman.

Nobody knows the troubles I've seen, except everyone who's ever been told to be one thing when they are another thing entirely.

Have you ever tried to make your body more congruent with what you've always felt yourself to be? Every culture and subculture has its own rules for what's a real man and what's a real woman, and for what's real desire and what's real sex. All I'm saying is we have a lot of work to do in order to define for ourselves what qualifies as real. We must find out which rules we've been breaking our spirits over trying to obey, and choose new rules that are self-loving. Blind, unconscious obedience to this culture's dream of a good-or-bad system of sexual desire is killing a lot of us, and that's no way or reason to die. It's the discovery of our individual desires beyond good-or-bad that makes a decent quality of life conceivable. Rather than killing ourselves, we could learn to kill off those parts of ourselves that are harmful.

Each one of us constructs various identities and personalities that we use in order to navigate our desires. Sometimes we don't do a very good job of it, and the identity we choose for ourselves—or the one that's been forced on us—just doesn't work or hurts other people. Such an identity needs to go so that we can continue our journey through the nature of our desire. The next time you just wanna die, kill off the part of you that got you into trouble *instead* and go on living as a whole new person. This is called the art of selective serial suicide.

It's how I try to consciously pick out all the stuff I don't like about myself and mark it for execution. It's the me who's mean, inconsiderate, greedy, and selfish. Those are the parts of me I wanna kill off, and I've been doing that consciously for nearly two decades. I've been killing off the parts of myself that need to die and making lots of room for all the parts of me that are beautiful and kind and life affirming. Do you do this already? Over the years, I've learned that the urge to kill myself isn't bad or wicked. It's scary, but it's just a signpost. It takes a long time to hone yourself down to the you that you've always believed you could be. For me, getting to the point of becoming what I'm attracted to has meant over fifty years of savage self-butchery.

Wouldn't you know, this noir survival tactic is built right into human biology in a little molecule called ubiquitin, your DNA's paid informant. It works sort of like this: The cells that make up our bodies are programmed to go into degradation mode whenever they stop functioning well. They eventually die and are replaced by new cells. But sometimes a cell in the body is malfunctioning and evading the body's natural degradation procedure. Fuck you, says

This is a drawing of the molecule ubiquitin.

this little cell, I'm gonna live, and I don't care who I take down with me, and it goes into hiding so that the body's natural SWAT team can't find and eliminate it. That's when they call in ubiquitin. As quick as you can say Judas Iscariot, ubiquitin locates the hidden part of your body that needs to die, and—get this—*kisses* the fugitive cell, marking it so that the execution easily follows. Blam! Your inner serial killer white blood cells are keeping you alive.

The next time you think you'd be better off dead than alive, please first look carefully to find the part of you that needs to die so that you can go on living. Ask yourself: Is there some identity you've constructed for yourself that keeps leading you into living a life that's not worth living? Are you acting out an identity that's been attracting the wrong sort of person into your life? Are you walking around in an identity that's gotten you completely off the path of your desire and onto someone else's path of desire?

If that's what's going on and it's enough to make you think about killing yourself, then build yourself a better identity, one that can be safer and free and enable you to have more fun. And if the you that needs to go refuses to die, then call in whatever version of ubiquitin appeals to you and kill the motherfucker. Use your favorite movie scene of sex and violence. Cast yourself as the assassin or vampire or whatever. Make it yummy and fun for both you and the you that you used to be. Give that death of yours some of the glory that our culture awards to sex and violence. All your yummy

dark sexual proclivities are fine and dandy. You just need to do something constructive with them. Then, wake up fresh as a daisy in the morning, ready for a life of conscious love.

I think our answers to the question, *Who am I?* can be approached on this path of conscious love, which is to say some combination of conscious desire, sex, and gender. We can learn to be conscious by taking any path we've previously been unconscious of: race, class, age . . . that whole laundry list of isms. Once you've learned how to be conscious along one of these paths, it's easier to learn consciousness along the others. The principles are transferable. I'm making a case for the paths of love, sex, and gender because too few people do, and too many people make a case against the serious study of our desire. And it is conscious desire and conscious gender that make it possible for me to feel sexy these days. So I'm wondering . . . I surely am a deeply flawed human being, but if I'm being kind then . . .

Does it matter who I fuck or how I fuck them?

Does it matter if I'm a man or a woman?

Does it matter if right this minute I'm neither?

And I wonder, for you. . .

Does it matter to you what you are: a man or a woman?

Does it matter to you who you're attracted to: men or women or both or neither?

I'm not saying it's a *bad* thing if any of this matters to you. It mattered to me for a lot of my life. I'm just asking you to think about why it's so important. It gets down to some real basic questions:

> *Would you like to be able to safely show the world the you that you most enjoy being?*
>
> *Would you like to be the sexiest you that you can be?*
>
> *Would you like to like your body and yourself?*

I think the real work starts with questions like these. There are people who've spent a great deal of their lives trying to find some answers. Your challenge is to find the kind ones and welcome them into your life so you can learn too, and to kindly pass *your* wisdom on to other folks. It takes practice to lovingly express your desire and to graciously accept or pass on someone else's.

I'd like to leave you with one of my favorite Zen principles: *the way you do anything is the way you do everything.* Everything you do is practice for everything else that you do. So, if you have ever desired something, anything—an ice cream cone or whatever—and then you made your own wish come true, that means you've got the means to make larger and larger wishes come true. Even the dreams you're told are bad but you know are harmless and wonderful. It takes practice, but you can make things happen for yourself. Just try to be kind to people and to yourself, and if that's too difficult, then try not to hurt anyone. Dreaming up and realizing a good life in a world that doesn't want you to have one, hey . . . that's good stuff, and you can do it.

for more good stuff on sex, turn to page 176 for hot sex tips and dating advice for young folk. woo-hoo!

PART 2

If you're thinking about killing yourself right this minute, and even if you're not, welcome to yet another day of trying to stay alive.

Hello, Cruel Quick-Start Guide

The best minds and kindest hearts in our culture would likely agree that the first seven options in this quick-start guide will help you to stop hurting so much. So, please try these before you move on to the less orthodox options listed in the 101 Alternatives to Suicide.

I've tried most of the following recommendations myself, and many of them worked very well. Predictably, some of them weren't the best choices for me. One or two seemed to make things worse, but left no permanent ill effect that I am aware of. Hands down, each of these steps is worth a shot before deciding to end your life. If they are just what you needed, you can read the rest of this book just for the funny parts.

If for any reason none of these more traditional alternatives sound right for you, or if you've already tried them and they just plain don't work and you're still on the razor's edge of to be or not to be, then by all means, move on to the rest of the book, which is neither proven nor condoned by those who've studied suicide prevention.

I. CALL A SUICIDE HOTLINE

A suicide hotline's job is to help you to feel better and live a little bit longer. If a warm voice on the other end of the telephone sounds like it might offer you some relief, then please give it a try.

II. TALK TO YOUR PAL

Do you know anyone you can talk to? Someone kind? Someone you love? Someone who loves you? If you can call or go see someone like that, please do! That, as they say, is what friends are for.

III. SEE A DOCTOR, THERAPIST, OR ALTERNATIVE HEALER

If what's going on with you is physical, then go see a doctor. If it's not a physical problem, give talking with a therapist or coun-selor a try. If a pill once or twice a day will help you feel better about life and yourself, then please, take the pill. I take mine.

In the case that the sight of you is enough to make men scream and strong women weep, try a clinic that is friendlier to people like you. I've always found clinic staff and doctors to be comforting and empowering. They've mostly seen it all. As a bonus, a lot of clinics are starting to provide alternative healing, which is great when Western medicine solutions give you the creeps.

IV. CALL THE POLICE OR EMERGENCY SERVICES

If someone has hurt you, or is threatening to hurt you, please call 911. There are also rape crisis centers, centers for battered youth, and other emergency centers where you may find good people with the experience and resources to help you out.

V. CALL SOMEONE WHO TAUGHT YOU SOMETHING YOU'LL ALWAYS TREASURE

I've been lucky enough to have had guidance counselors, teachers, professors, and even a couple of chaplains of several religions who've cared enough about me to hold my hand through some pretty tough times. I'm still friends with some of them after thirty or forty years. Is there a teacher like that in your life?

Depending on their own personal moral code, or on local and state laws where you live, a teacher or member of the clergy may or may not be required to report your situation to someone authorized to know and help you out. Ask them first if that's the case, and make your decision accordingly.

VI. GET TO A MEETING!

If you think you might have any sort of addiction, this would be a swell time to get to a twelve-step meeting. Most of the time, the idea of going to a meeting sets my teeth on edge, and makes me want to run screaming in the other direction. But honestly, I don't regret any twelve-step meeting I've ever attended, and if you've got any kind of sobriety, you know I'm telling the truth.

VII. CONNECT WITH PEOPLE ONLINE

If you don't have your own Internet connection, find someone else's you can use. Your school, the public library, a friend, or an Internet café are all possibilities that you might want to look into.

There are online peer chat rooms, forums, and bulletin boards where people discuss the subject of killing themselves, or how other people are killing themselves. There are websites and blogs dedicated to suicide intervention. Someone out there is going to want to talk with you about this and they may say just the right thing to make you feel better about yourself and your life.

Are You Still a Mess?

Okay, it's time to try the road less sanctioned.

I'm done trying to steer you toward socially-sanctioned methods of stopping yourself from ending your life. If none of this has worked for you, or if any of it sounded wrong or frightening, there are some options that have not necessarily been sanctioned by therapists and medical doctors. I have not studied the subject for years, but I've got the suicide survivor equivalent of street smarts because I'm an outsider, and most of the sanctioned solutions weren't always available to me each time my life took another giddy turn toward self-destruction.

THE CATCH

No single alternative I've found to killing myself has ever been enough to keep me alive for longer than a year or so. From therapy and self-affirmations to drugs and self-injury, it worked only for a while. Inevitably, whatever I was doing would slowly or suddenly stop working, and I'd have to move on to some other way to get back in touch with a good reason to keep on going. Some of the methods I've used to stay alive have only worked for a few hours, or a few minutes.

THE MEAN REDS

"Listen . . . you know those days when you get the mean reds? The blues are because you're getting fat, or because it's been raining too long. You're just sad, that's all. The mean reds are horrible. Suddenly you're afraid and you don't know what you're afraid of. Do you ever get that feeling? When I get it the only thing that does any good is to jump into a cab and go to Tiffany's. Calms me down right away." —MISS HOLLY GOLIGHTLY

When I was still a guy, I moved to New York, and at the first bout of the mean reds, went right down to Tiffany's and had breakfast by the window, and sure enough, it worked! But that was years ago, and now Tiffany's isn't as elegant as it was back when Mr. Capote wrote his novella. So maybe instead of Tiffany's, you can find yourself a lovely place or head space that makes you feel completely safe and well-cared for.

Life is suffering."

—The Buddha

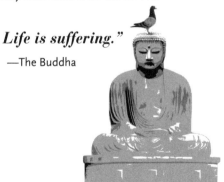

BONUS BRAIN TEASER PAGE!

Here are a few of my favorite horrible things the mean reds have given me to suffer through. How many do you suppose we have in common, you and I?

Those times when I had nowhere to go, nothing to do, and no one to tell it all to.

Those times when I was lonely to the bone, but there was no one I felt safe or comfortable enough to be with.

Those times when I was so physically sick and hurting that I couldn't even imagine getting better.

Those times when I was so depressed, or in such despair or terror, that I couldn't even imagine happiness.

Those times when I was full to the brim with tears, but I couldn't cry even though I wanted to.

Those times when I couldn't stand what I was, and I didn't know how I could possibly be something else.

Those times when I could no longer stand living where I was living, but there was nowhere else I particularly wanted to go, and no way to get there anyhow.

Those times when I felt I couldn't go on living with someone, but I couldn't imagine my life without them.

Those times when I felt terribly guilty, or just plain wrong, about doing something, but I was sure I'd only feel worse if I stopped doing it.

Those times when I hated how I was being treated, but I didn't see that there was anything I could do about it.

Those times when I didn't want to go on living any more, but it made me even more depressed and immobilized to think about killing myself.

For me, staying alive through all that and more has come down to this:

1. I FIGURE OUT WHAT IT IS THAT I'M FEELING.

I have to figure out where I am before I can figure out where to go, or how to get there. Often, all I feel is BAD. From there, I have to figure out what kind of BAD I'm feeling.

2. I CHOOSE A BETTER FEELING, AND PUT IT IN MOTION.

I'm not talking about finding a way to feel *happy*. I'm talking about finding a way to feel *better* than the way you feel right now. Happy/sad is a binary that mostly keeps us stuck in sad. We can't seem to get happy except for when we're not looking for happiness, and the only other option seems to be sad. So, in this step, I look for a feeling that is closer to happy than where I am at the moment.

3. I FIGURE OUT WHAT TO DO NEXT, AND MAKE PREPARATIONS.

What's working for you *now* may not work for you after you've changed something about yourself. It's like needing a new version of software after a system upgrade. I aim to begin my *new* way to feel better before my *old* one stops working.

I do all of that over and over and over again. Ain't life grand?

Keep doing whatever it is that's working for you.

Over the course of your life, you've already worked out several ways to live that make you want to live more. First, I'm going to invite you to do more of that. What was the last thing you did that made life worth living? And if that option is now gone, what were you doing to stay alive before that? And before that?

Let's take a little peek inside your heart. I'm going to bet that happy is a long way away from where you are right now. But *happy* is a poor word for someone who's trying to live a rainbow-colored life in a black-and-white world. *Bad* is another poor word to describe how you're feeling. A large part of learning how to enjoy life is learning how to identify your emotions, and how to foster the particular ones that lead you toward joy.

So, what are you feeling right now?

What might be a better feeling you could aim for?

How about a better feeling you've actually got a prayer in hell of realizing?

On the next page, you'll find a scale of feelings and emotions that will aid you in naming what it is that you're feeling. You'll be able to scratch out the words you disagree with and write in better words for yourself later, but for now try to work with this list.

If you're considering killing yourself, you're probably going to be somewhere on the right-hand side of the page. You want to lead yourself to somewhere on the left-hand side of the page.

HELLO, CRUEL SCALE OF FEELINGS

1. Joy, wisdom
2. Love, freedom
3. Passion

4. Empowerment
5. Positive expectation, belief
6. Delight

7. Satisfaction, contentment
8. Appreciation
9. Optimism, cheerfulness
10. Hopefulness

11. Pessimism
12. Irritation
13. Frustration
14. Feeling overwhelmed

15. Disappointment
16. Doubt
17. Worry, the blues
18. Blame
19. Discouragement

20. Anger
21. Vengefulness
22. Rage, hatred
23. Jealousy

24. Guilt, shame
25. Uselessness
26. Grief, loneliness

27. Fear, terror, the mean reds
28. Depression, despair
29. Hopelessness, feeling trapped

How do you find where you might fall on the scale? Here's a good way to spot your current position:

Scan the list either from the bottom up or the top down, and stop when you get to a word that describes what you're feeling. Look at a few feelings within the same group and choose the one that's *most* descriptive of how you feel.

If the first step is to locate yourself on the scale, the next is to choose a feeling that is closer to joy. Much higher than the same group or the next group up isn't too likely to happen overnight. American culture is obsessed with tackling things in leaps and bounds. Take little steps, please. You'll feel better. Steady baby steps will get you a lot more surely where you want to go, with a great deal more satisfaction and self-confidence.

Have you picked out a feeling that's better than the one you've got right now?

Then, it's time to determine a way to get there.

No one can tell you how you feel. No one. But, a kind soul can help you to figure out for yourself how you feel. And because you're the only one who can know, it is pretty important that you do.

The meat and potatoes of this book is the list of 101 Alternatives to Suicide designed to keep you from plummeting down the scale of emotions.

Using the index on pages 100–106, find and explore any of the 101 Alternatives that you think might help you feel a little bit better than you are feeling right now. Each alternative is also ranked in a number of categories to help you navigate the best ones for you. There's no right or wrong choice, I swear. If several alternatives look good to you, I suggest you select the one that has the most hearts (which indicates it's the safest and most self-loving alternative) and sounds like the easiest, or most fun.

What's a Positive Feeling, and What's a Negative?

Pessimism might seem out of place well over half-way up the scale. But it makes sense when you look at it closely. Despite their sour expectations, pessimists are trying to get something done, and I'd say that's healthier than not trying at all.

And what about anger? I think anger is a whole lot more positive a feeling than depression. I feel a lot healthier when I'm angry than when I'm paralyzed in a deep funk. Other people around me might prefer me when I'm not flying off the handle, but most folks who know me now appreciate that my anger is a step up my own personal ladder to feeling better.

I hate being lonely, but loneliness would be a better feeling for me than, say, hopelessness. To my way of thinking, anger and loneliness are a lot closer to being free to live the kind of life that I'd want to stay alive in. To me, motion toward freedom, joy, wisdom, and love would define what's positive. Accordingly, motion toward immobility, slavery, despair and death define the negative.

YOU CAN TELL THEM
THE DEVIL MADE YOU DO IT

Over the course of this book, I will be giving you permission to do anything you want to do—anything at all—short of killing yourself. I don't care if it's illegal, immoral, fattening, self-defeating, whatever. I'm going to say go ahead, because I've done it myself. However, my permission is worthless if you can't give *yourself* permission. I'll show you a couple of ways to give yourself permission to do anything at all that you want to do, as long as it isn't mean to anyone.

Being mean triggers shame and regret, not to mention bad karma. Shame and regret are nature's way of telling us to forgive ourselves for whatever we just did, apologize and make amends for it if we can, and try to do better next time. That's how we learn to be kind as we keep on in life's journey. No one is perfectly kind, compassionate, and generous. But you can live a kinder, more compassionate, and generous life by following just one simple rule: DON'T BE MEAN. Anything else goes, anything at all.

I've done my best to warn you about any legal, moral, or health hazards connected with any of the alternatives that I suggest you do. But here's the deal: even though I've done a lot of it myself, yer on yer own just like I've been on my own when it comes to any illegal stuff. I'll feel bad for you, but there's nothing I can do to help you with that one. And nothing in this book should ever be interpreted as suggesting that you be mean to anyone. So, with these conditions firmly in place, if anyone gives you any trouble over anything I suggest you do that isn't mean to anyone, show them this:

I'll do your time in Hell for you. Yup. Just don't be mean, and if you get sent to Hell for anything I'm suggesting in this book, you show the Devil this Get Out of Hell Free Card. Aren't I a peach? So, what are you waiting for? Check out the 101 Alternatives for Teens, Freaks and Other Outlaws.

101 Alternatives to Suicide

FOR TEENS, FREAKS AND OTHER OUTLAWS

KEY

HOW EASY IS IT TO DO?

(EACH ALTERNATIVE RATED ON A DIFFICULTY SCALE)

As easy as petting a cow

As tricky as riding a cow

As difficult as a cow on wheels

Real easy and real dangerous

Thanks for all the cows go to DOMA.tv in Argentina, for the cool freeware font, DOMA Originals.

HOW SAFE IS IT?
(EACH ALTERNATIVE RATED ON A FOUR HEART SCALE)

HOW EFFECTIVE IS IT?
(EACH ALTERNATIVE RATED ON A FOUR UMBRELLA SCALE)

The more hearts, the safer and more self-loving the alternative. The more skulls, the less safe and self-loving. Each alternative is rated on a four-heart and four-skull scale.

The more umbrellas, the more effective it will be, four being the highest number of umbrellas possible. Why use a less effective option? Because it will be somewhat effective, and it might be just the thing to make you feel a little bit better, and help you in your transition to more positive feelings.

Thank you to Googe & King Buffalo Graphics for the great free Skullz font.

IS IT MORE OR LESS LEGAL AND MORAL?

G   General. Anyone can do it, even your grandma. You could even talk about doing this in front of your parents or your boss if you wanted to.

YG   Youth Guidance. Don't try this alternative unless you've run it by, or are accompanied by, a youth.

YG-50 Youth Guidance mandatory for anyone over fifty. If you're over fifty, don't try to read this option without a youth present. It wouldn't make much sense to you. Really. I'm over fifty, and I've been listening to a lot of youth explain things to me. It helps.

X   No one older than Gen-X should attempt, or even read, this option.

ASS   Adult Supervision Suggested.

I'm not trying to be cute with these ratings. Well, yes I am. But this is a valid way to size up which alternative you think might get you to the next step up on your emotional journey toward joy and wisdom.

INDEX OF ALTERNATIVES

ALTERNATIVE	SAFETY	HOW EFFECTIVE	HOW DIFFICULT	RATING	KEYWORDS
1. Keep moving.	♥♥♥☠	☂☂☂☂	Tricky	G	real life, spirit, body
2. Take a deep breath and touch yourself	♥♥♥♥	☂☂☂☂	Easy	G	spirit, body, delight
3. Kill some time instead	♥♥♥♥	☂☂☂☂	Easy	G	comfort, spirit
4. Treat yourself like an honored guest	♥♥♥♥	☂☂☂☂	Difficult	G	comfort, self-esteem
5. Finish your homework first.	♥♥♥♥	☂☂☂☂	Difficult	YG	safety, rehearsal
6. Just say no.	♥♥♥☠	☂☂☂☂	Tricky	G	empowering, self-esteem
7. Trash your preference files and reboot.	♥♥☠☠	☂☂	Tricky	G	clean slate
8. Practice, Practice, Practice	♥♥♥♥	☂☂☂☂	Easy	G	spirit, rehearsal
9. Make a longer-range plan.	♥♥♥♥	☂☂☂☂	Tricky	G	real life
10 Bitch, moan, rant or rave.	♥♥♥☠	☂☂☂	Easy	G	comfort
11. Tell a lie.	♥☠☠☠	☂☂	Too Easy	G	safety, entertainment
12. Send out a distress signal.	♥♥☠☠	☂☂	Tricky	G	hope, faith, self-esteem
13. Ask for help.	♥♥♥☠	☂☂☂	Difficult	G	spirit, real life
14. Run away and hide.	♥♥♥♥	☂☂☂	Difficult	G	safety, real life
15. Run a diagnostic program.	♥♥♥♥	☂☂☂☂	Tricky	G	safety, real life

ALTERNATIVE	SAFETY	HOW EFFECTIVE	HOW DIFFICULT	RATING	KEYWORDS
16. Find out what you look like.	♥♥♥♥	☂☂☂☂	Difficult	YG/ASS	self-esteem, body, relief
17. Make a deal with the Devil.	♥☠☠☠	☂☂	Tricky	G	mind game, comfort
18. Make 'em laugh.	♥♥♥☠	☂☂☂☂	Tricky	G	safety, delight, mischief
19. Make art out of it.	♥♥☠☠	☂☂☂☂	Tricky	G	real life, spirit, mischief
20. Sell the stuff you make.	♥♥♥♥	☂☂☂☂	Tricky	G	empowering, real life
21. Deal with the dead and gone.	♥♥♥☠	☂☂☂☂	Difficult	G/ASS	comfort
22. Moisturize!	♥♥♥♥	☂☂☂☂	Easy	G	comfort, delight, body
23. See yourself in everyone you meet.	♥♥♥♥	☂☂☂☂	Easy	G	delight, rehearsal
24. Save the whales, the children or the world.	♥♥♥☠	☂☂	Easy	G	comfort, purpose
25. Experiment on animals and small children.	♥♥♥♥	☂☂☂☂	Tricky	YG	delight, rehearsal, body
26. Join a group that wants you as a member, or start one of your own.	♥♥☠☠	☂☂	Easy	G	comfort
27. Give 'em the old razzle dazzle.	♥♥☠☠	☂☂☂☂	Tricky	G	safety, magic, mischief
28. Give yourself permission.	♥♥♥☠	☂☂☂	Tricky	G	empowering, real life, spirit
29. Play a game you like to play.	♥♥☠☠	☂☂☂	Difficult	G	clean slate, delight

ALTERNATIVE	SAFETY	HOW EFFECTIVE	HOW DIFFICULT	RATING	KEYWORDS
30. Get out there and be a star!	♥💀💀💀	⬆	Difficult	YG-50	thrill ride
31. Get out there and be an extra!	♥♥♥💀	⬆⬆⬆	Easy	G	delight, real life, comfort
32. Get out there and be an ex.	♥♥♥♥	⬆⬆⬆	Easy	G	empowering, purpose
33. Stop fucking around and get to work.	♥♥♥♥	⬆⬆⬆⬆	Difficult	G	real life, empowering
34. Sing for your supper.	♥♥💀💀	⬆⬆⬆	Difficult	G	real life, spirit, purpose
35. Dance for your life.	♥💀💀💀	⬆	Difficult	G	safety
36. Kill every last one of those mother-fuckers. (Okay, not really.)	♥♥♥♥	⬆⬆	Easy	G	thrill ride, relief, mind game
37. Keep moving on.	♥💀💀💀	⬆⬆⬆	Difficult	G	clean slate
38. Cast a spell.	♥♥💀💀	⬆⬆⬆	Tricky	G	magic, safety
39. Make a wish.	♥♥💀💀	⬆⬆⬆	Tricky	G	spirit, magic, purpose
40. Make believe.	♥♥♥♥	⬆⬆⬆	Easy	G	comfort, purpose, rehearsal
41. Make a dream come true for someone else.	♥♥♥♥	⬆⬆⬆⬆	Easy	G	delight, purpose
42. Act your age or any other.	♥♥♥💀	⬆⬆⬆	Easy	YG/ASS	real life, empowering, mischief
43. Act your gender or any other.	♥♥💀💀	⬆⬆⬆	Tricky	YG-50	comfort, delight, empowering
44. Use the wrong tool for the job.	♥♥💀💀	⬆⬆	Tricky	YG/ASS	real life, mischief
45. Come out, come out, whatever you are.	♥💀💀💀	⬆⬆⬆⬆	Tricky	YG/ASS	empowering, delight, purpose

ALTERNATIVE	SAFETY	HOW EFFECTIVE	HOW DIFFICULT	RATING	KEYWORDS
46. Find the love of your life.	♥☠☠☠	⇧	Difficult	G	thrill ride, body, delight
47. Find a friend.	♥♥♥☠	⇧⇧⇧⇧	Tricky	G	real life, comfort, safety
48. Find your tribe	♥♥♥☠	⇧⇧⇧	Tricky	G	comfort, relief, safety
49. Find a God who believes in you.	♥♥♥♥	⇧⇧⇧⇧	Tricky	G	comfort, magic, spirit
50. Be your own hero/ine.	♥♥♥♥	⇧⇧⇧⇧	Easy	G	delight, empowering, real life
51. Be your own evil twin.	♥♥☠☠	⇧⇧	Easy	G	safety, real life, mischief
52. Become a more frightening monster than the one they think you are.	♥♥☠☠	⇧⇧⇧	Tricky	G	mischief, delight, magic
53. Be cute or be dashing.	♥♥♥☠	⇧⇧	Tricky	G	delight, empowering, body
54. Be afraid. Be very afraid.	♥♥♥♥	⇧⇧⇧⇧	Tricky	G	empowering, clean slate, purpose
55. Be orgasmically celibate.	♥♥♥♥	⇧⇧⇧⇧	Tricky	G	delight, comfort, body
56. Get laid. Please.	♥♥♥♥	⇧⇧⇧⇧	Tricky	G	delight, comfort, body
57. Say please and thank you.	♥♥☠☠	⇧⇧⇧	Easy	G	mischief, thrill ride, delight
58. Serve somebody.	♥♥☠☠	⇧⇧⇧	Tricky	G	purpose, delight, rehearsal
59. Eroticize the pain.	♥☠☠☠	⇧⇧	Tricky	G	comfort, delight
60. Bake a cake.	♥♥♥♥	⇧⇧⇧⇧	Tricky	G	delight
61. Eat it all.	♥♥☠☠	⇧	Too Easy	G	comfort, if you must
62. Stay in bed.	♥♥♥♥	⇧⇧⇧	Easy	G	comfort

ALTERNATIVE	SAFETY	HOW EFFECTIVE	HOW DIFFICULT	RATING	KEYWORDS
63. Travel and have adventures.	♥♡♡♡	↑↑↑↑	Tricky	G	empowering, spirit, thrill ride
64. Go on a quest	♥♡♡♡	↑↑↑↑	Difficult	G	empowering, spirit, purpose
65. Go shopping	♥♡♡♡	↑	Easy	G	comfort
66. Go stealth.	♥♥♡♡	↑↑	Tricky	YG	safety, delight, comfort
67. Go for it against all odds.	♥♡♡♡	↑↑↑↑	Difficult	G	thrill ride, empowering, purpose
68. Go completely batty.	♡♡♡♡	↑↑	Too Easy	ASS	safety, comfort, if you must
69. Go on a serial suicide spree.	♥♥♡♡	↑↑↑↑	Tricky	YG	spirit, clean slate, empowering
70. Get a makeover.	♥♥♡♡	↑↑↑	Tricky	YG	delight, clean slate, comfort
71. Geek out.	♥♥♥♡	↑↑↑	Difficult	G	real life, empowering, comfort
72. Give up nouns for a day.	♥♥♥♥	↑↑↑↑	Tricky	G	mind game, spirit, delight
73. Make a name for yourself in the world.	♥♥♡♡	↑↑↑	Tricky	G	safety, empowering, thrill ride
74. Frame your own debate	♥♥♥♡	↑↑↑	Difficult	G	purpose, mischief, mind game
75. Use another word for hello.	♥♥♥♥	↑↑↑	Difficult	G	delight, spirit, real world
76. Learn another language of love.	♥♥♥♥	↑↑↑↑	Difficult	YG/ASS	spirit, delight, safety
77. Flirt with Death.	♡♡♡♡	↑↑	Too Easy	YG/ASS	thrill ride, spirit, if you must
78. Make it bleed.	♥♡♡♡	↑↑↑↑	Too Easy	YG-50	relief, if you must
79. Take drugs. No, really. Take drugs.	♥♡♡♡	↑↑↑	Too Easy	YG	if you must

ALTERNATIVE	SAFETY	HOW EFFECTIVE	HOW DIFFICULT	RATING	KEYWORDS
80. Get sort of clean and sober.	♥♡♡♡	☂	Difficult	G	if you must
81. Starve yourself	♡♡♡♡	☂	Too Easy	G	if you must
82. Play musical addictions.	♥♡♡♡	☂	Tricky	G	if you must, thrill ride
83. Plead insanity.	♥♥♥♥	☂☂☂☂	Difficult	YG/ASS	safety, delight, mischief
84. Defy prophecy	♥♥♥♡	☂☂☂☂	Tricky	G	clean slate, purpose, relief
85. Throw away morals.	♥♥♡♡	☂☂☂☂	Tricky	YG/ASS	self-esteem, relief, mischief
86. Ignore the Golden Rule.	♥♥♥♡	☂☂☂	Tricky	G	empowering, spirit
87. Quote scripture for your own purposes	♥♡♡♡	☂	Tricky	G	mischief, empowering
88. Write your own code of honor.	♥♥♡♡	☂☂☂☂	Tricky	G	empowering, real life, purpose
89. Shatter some family values.	♥♥♡♡	☂☂☂	Tricky	G	spirit, empowering, mischief
90. Believe in your own laughter.	♥♥♥♥	☂☂☂☂	Easy	G	delight, body, relief
91. Believe in your own paradox.	♥♥♥♡	☂☂☂☂	Difficult	G	spirit, delight, mind game
92. Choose your battles wisely.	♥♥♡♡	☂☂☂☂	Tricky	YG/ASS	safety, empowering, purpose
93. Bring on Goliath.	♥♡♡♡	☂☂☂☂	Difficult	YG/ASS	safety, purpose, clean slate
94. Speak with your ears.	♥♥♥♡	☂☂☂	Tricky	G	spirit, purpose, empowering
95. Play to a broader audience.	♥♥♡♡	☂☂	Difficult	G	purpose, real life, safety
96. Take a vow of silence.	♥♥♥♥	☂☂☂☂	Difficult	G	comfort, real life

ALTERNATIVE	SAFETY	HOW EFFECTIVE	HOW DIFFICULT	RATING	KEYWORDS
97. Take a walk in the woods.	♥♥♥♥	👆👆👆👆	Easy	G	body, comfort, spirit
98. Learn moderation in all things.	♥♥♥♥	👆👆👆👆	Tricky	G	real life, comfort, spirit
99. Make your peace with Death.	♥♥♥♥	👆👆👆👆	Difficult	G	real life, comfort, spirit
100. Tidy your campsite before you move on.	♥♥♥♥	👆👆👆👆	Tricky	YG/ASS	clean slate, spirit, comfort
101. Try to keep someone else alive.	♥♥♥♥	👆👆👆👆	Tricky	G	delight, comfort, relief

KEYWORDS: spiritual, body, real life

G

Do you ever get stir crazy, like you can't stand being where you are any longer? Do you know how good it feels to finally get out of there? Less and less movement is a sign of less and less life. Dead things don't move at all. Any kind of motion means there's some life. Learning how to move well will help you learn how to live better.

The process of living can be reduced to a simple series of acts: deciding to move, moving, deciding to stop, and stopping. You can move with the intention of feeling better, and you can move with the intention of feeling worse. Moving through life with the intention of feeling better is what's going to make life worth living for you.

TRY THIS: Do something as slowly as you can, or do nothing as quickly as you can. Take thirty minutes to get yourself across the room, without ever coming to a complete stop. If you can't get yourself across the room, take thirty minutes to imagine yourself doing it.

FOLLOW UP WITH THESE: Once you've got the hang of constant conscious motion and constant change, try #29, Play a game you *like* to play or #64, Go on a quest.

RECOMMENDED: The book *On the Road* by Jack Kerouac; the episode "Out of Gas" from the TV show *Firefly*; and the film *Finding Nemo*. Listen to the music you most enjoy moving to.

2. TAKE A DEEP BREATH AND TOUCH YOURSELF

KEYWORDS: spirit, body, delight

Would you like to feel a miracle? Our bodies are miraculous, no matter what shape they're in. Consciously breathing and touching ourselves reminds us that it's possible to feel better. When we don't know how to describe what it is that we're feeling, our bodies will always tell us the truth of the situation. We so often hold our bodies responsible for our bad fortune that we forget how good they feel when we treat them well.

So, breathe. If you want to calm yourself, breathe in through your nose and out through your mouth. For lots of air, breathe in and out through your mouth. Don't force your exhales, just let them happen. Pay attention to your breathing over the course of a day. There's a great deal to learn from the truth of your own body.

THE RESILIENT EDGE OF RESISTANCE: Press your palm onto the back of your other hand. Press your hands together, using pressure from both. Now, let the pressure lighten up until it doesn't feel like you're pressing them together, but that they're supporting each other. This is what my girlfriend calls "the resilient edge of resistance." Touching yourself or someone else with this principle in mind can really change things in your life.

ADVANCED MODE: Touch yourself while you're breathing. Anywhere. Just consciously touch yourself, and feel what it feels like. That's all. Anywhere on your body that's comfortable for you, touch. Keep breathing!

WAY-ADVANCED MODE: Breathe and touch yourself erotically, anywhere on your body. Just use the resilient edge of resistance (see sidebar), and discover what feels good and what feels bad. Give yourself an orgasm if the opportunity comes up and you're feeling okay about that. Orgasms are great for getting rid of bad headaches and most general grumpiness.

DID YOU KNOW Orgasms come from more places than just your genitals. You can make yourself come with your breath. Over and over again, as a matter of fact. I swear! It's great. I learned how from some experts.

RECOMMENDED: Any books, DVDs, or audio tapes by Annie Sprinkle, Barbara Carrellas (my girlfriend!), Joseph Kramer, or Chester Mainard.

3. KILL SOME TIME INSTEAD.

G

KEYWORDS: comfort, spiritual

Under pressure? Never have enough time to complete everything that you have to do? If time is pushing you around, kill it. Time, the way it's served up to us here by puritanical corporate America, needs to die anyway. It's far too demanding and gives you very little in return, even if you make the very most of it. After we kill off that kind of time, we can use time differently so that life isn't such a pressure cooker.

Here are some surefire time killers I use whenever I possibly can:

I take a nap.

I observe a Sabbath.

I use some of my own time to be kind to someone else.

RECOMMENDED: *Sabbath: Finding Rest, Renewal, and Delight in Our Busy Lives* by Wayne Muller.

An advanced time-killer: Sit with your eyes closed for three minutes. If the only place you can do this for three whole uninterrupted minutes is the bathroom, then scoot there now and bring this book with you. Sit still with your eyes closed for three whole minutes, and witness your thoughts go by. Try not to engage in any kind of dialogue with your thoughts, just watch them pass. If it helps, you can envision a thought floating into and out of your mind on a cloud. Even thunderclouds pass by eventually. See if you can increase the amount of time you spend doing this.

4. TREAT YOURSELF LIKE AN HONORED GUEST.

KEYWORDS: comfort, self-esteem

Around the world and across the ages, there's something nice that most humans and other sentient beings agree upon: when you've got guests, you treat them well. You wouldn't beat up on a guest you'd welcomed into your home, would you?

Do you beat up on yourself much? Well, then stop. If you show up on the culture's radar as some sort of visible freak or outsider, you end up building your own world to walk through, so the very least you can do is make yourself feel welcome in that world. Try it out: spend one day living like you're some visiting dignitary in a world that welcomes and celebrates people like you. That's what living your life is *supposed* to feel like, no matter

In Shakespeare's *Macbeth*, the true horror wasn't that the Macbeths killed the king. That happened all the time. Their great offense was in killing the king while he was a guest in their home. That's why the Macbeths were not at first suspected of the crime. Who would suspect anyone of being so low? Everyone deserves to feel cared for, respected, and welcome. So, shouldn't we learn how to do that for ourselves?

what kind of freak or outsider other people might think you are.

Do something really special for yourself. Something really nice, like a bubble bath or a piece of chocolate with fresh fruit. It's important to do that every now and then to remind yourself how nice it feels to be welcome and well cared for.

PRACTICE MODE: If treating yourself better is difficult to do, or even imagine doing, use #25, Experiment on animals and small children, and practice treating *them* like honored guests.

5. FINISH YOUR HOMEWORK FIRST.

KEYWORDS: safety, rehearsal

Schooling designed to make a sweeping, impersonal system work sucks. It is not at all tailored to your individual interests, strengths, or talents. It can make life not worth living.

But it's not learning that's getting you down. It's getting through an educational *system*. So, work the system, change the system, or leave it, but make sure you keep on educating yourself, and as many other people as you can.

The good news is that that no such system is the boss of you. You can have great autonomy in the things you choose to learn and pursue on your own time. When you're learning things that interest you, challenge you, and make life worth living, getting an education can be blissful and stimulating.

There's only one thing to do: your homework. Do you have a

favorite field of interest? Biology? Math? History? Computer science? Give yourself assignments in that field, and exercise your mind. Treat yourself like the teacher you always wanted to have.

ENDURANCE MODE: Get to college, any college. Well, maybe not Bible College. But get to college by any means possible. Search for and find a field of study that makes you really happy and excited to be learning. Search for and find a mentor who helps you in your studies. Stay for years.

NEUROGENETIC MODE: Learn something new. It helps you grow new brain cells. Is that cool, or what? According to the decade-old field of neurogenesis, stress inhibits the growth of new brain cells, forming scars on our brains and causing depression. Simply learning something new helps to heal those scars, so we feel better. Yippee!

REVOLUTIONARY MODE: School yourself. Speak with other self-schoolers who are doing the kind of things you want to be doing, and get on with teaching yourself about whatever part of life is calling you. I don't have an advanced degree beyond my B.A., but my books get taught in doctoral programs. It all works out.

RECOMMENDED: *The Teenage Liberation Handbook* by Grace Llewellyn, *Jefferson's Children* by Leon Botstein, and *A Whole New Mind* by Daniel Pink.

6. JUST SAY NO.

KEYWORDS: empowering, self-esteem

Saying no to something bad now will always let you say yes to something better later. But standing up and saying no can also make you an instantly recognizable freak, and a target to the people who want you to say yes to something that is hurting you and/or others.

No, I don't want to wear a dress,

No, I don't want to play football,

No, I refuse to support the criminally mean activities of an illegitimate, quasi-fascist corporate government.

I've never been more proud of myself than at those times I've said no when I needed to. But saying no is just the first step. Acting on no is the second, and the third, and every other step along the way.

There are alternatives to saying no when no is too hard to say. You could simply not say yes. That's called passive resistance. Check out the M. K. Gandhi Institute for Nonviolence (www.gandhiinstitute.org).

Or, you could get yourself out of the reach of whoever you want to say no to. The Dalai Lama says no to China's occupation of Tibet like that (www.tibet.com).

You could even run away and hide and get yourself stronger, like Linda Hamilton in *Terminator II*. See #14, Run away and hide.

ADVANCED MODE: Use #93, Bring on Goliath, to say no to someone who's been intimidating you for too long.

7. TRASH YOUR PREFERENCE FILES AND REBOOT.

KEYWORDS: empowering, self-esteem

Outsiders go through quite a few identities, each with its own set of preferences for dealing with different situations. We can change our conscious preferences easily enough, but sometimes it can help to change the things we do habitually or unconsciously as well.

Try this: For three or four days, write down the little things you do that you normally don't think about doing, including any morning, afternoon, or evening routines, any habits you've got, your daily chores, how you deal with things that bore or annoy you, and the kind of music you're listening to most. Write down ten things you find yourself thinking about without your having chosen to think about them. Notice how you answer questions like "How are you?" and "How was your day?"

Now you're ready to shut down and reboot. For three days, no TV, radio, internet, music, film, games, newspapers, magazines, and so forth. You can talk with people, but no communication with anything that can't speak back to you of its own intelligence. Be as aware as you possibly can of everything you say or do on a moment-to-moment basis, and try to make conscious, informed choices about what you say and what you do, without relying on the kind of choices you used to make. Make your new preference files as pristinely your own as they can possibly be.

TIP: Keep a copy of your old preferences in your conscious memory files. Then you'll have a copy to put back in place in case you trash any good preferences by accident. It always pays to back up your files!

HERMIONE MODE: Use this alternative along with #38, Cast a spell, to devise and perform a cleansing and grounding ritual for yourself.

8. PRACTICE, PRACTICE, PRACTICE.

   G

KEYWORDS: spirit, rehearsal

This may be the key to the whole fucking book. Practicing *anything* will keep you more conscious, honest, and more capable of laughing at yourself. It's based on the Zen principle, *the way you do anything is the way you do everything.*

To get good at something, we usually practice until we know how to do it well. Like walking, talking, eating, or even fucking. Once something works, the things we do become unconscious habits or mindless routines. Like checking our email, doing our laundry, reading the paper, or even fucking. But because the way you do anything is the way you do everything, every single thing you do *could* be a conscious rehearsal for how you do everything else. *Especially* fucking.

Practice doing things more consciously. Before you start doing things, become aware of your intention to do them. Notice the difference between your intention to do something you already know how to do well, and your intention to do something you don't yet know how to do well.

Try to consciously perform one task well every day. It doesn't have to be something new or dramatic. Just do one thing consciously and well at least once a day.

RECOMMENDED: *How You Do Anything Is How You Do Everything: A Workbook* by Cheri Huber. Practical Zen meets postmodern theory meets earth mom.

9. MAKE LONGER-RANGE PLANS.

KEYWORDS: real life

G

Feeling hopeless? Make a plan, any plan. Plan your day. Plan how you're going to get out of bed. Plan how you'll take over the world. Making plans builds up our hopes, and once we've got a glimmer of hope, we've got a reason to go on living. You can build up your hopes right now by making really simple plans.

When I was twelve years old, I wanted to be a girl. I knew there was no chance of ever making that happen, but my daydreams were enjoyable enough in themselves to make life worth living. In retrospect, my young fantasies were what allowed me to develop a goal and a plan to achieve it, even though I thought it was unachievable. Now, I see building hope as an essential and pleasurable step toward realization.

Try planning what the next fifteen minutes of your life will be like. When you're done making the plan, see if you are more or less interested in living. Do you feel a little better about life now that you have a plan? See how that works? Making the plan is as fun and as important as achieving it. The way the world works, many of our plans won't pan out. There's always some random element that we can't predict. And if our plans include other people? Ha! The best we can do is start the plan in motion and then hang on and enjoy the ride. So, try putting less importance on whether or not your plans succeed. Have more fun making them.

ADVANCED MODE: See #19, Make art out of it, and become an endurance artist. That's an artist who specializes in pieces that can last for days, months, and even years. Imagine living your life as art for all that time! For more on just how to do that, read *Letters from Linda M. Montano* edited by Jennie Klein. Give the rest of us lessons.

WAY-ADVANCED MODE: See #91, Believe in your own paradox, and live fully in the now, at peace with your past and accomplishing your dream of a better future.

10. RANT, RAVE, BITCH, AND MOAN.

KEYWORD: comfort

G

Oh, go for it. Give voice to your inner drama queen. You know you want to.

Dogs and cats make great listeners. So do understanding lovers and best friends. The best person to bitch, moan, rant, or rave to is a person who will let you keep on going until you're done. Just take care not to aim your drama at your friends and loved ones. And if you're afraid you might overburden or frighten them with all your pathetic whimpering and hostile growling, try this: Set yourself a reasonable time limit, and mark it on a calendar. When your time's up, stop bitching and moaning and try #19, Make art out of it.

RECOMMENDED: This alternative is dedicated to the master of radical outlaw angry comedy Diane DiMassa, the artist who created Hothead Paisan: Homicidal Lesbian Terrorist. Get the complete works and watch your anger melt away!

11. TELL A LIE.

   G

KEYWORDS: safety, entertainment

First, the bad news. Lying always comes back to bite you on your butt. Telling a lie almost always triggers a string of more lies to cover up the first. And when you lie to someone, you almost always damage the trust they have in you. That said, where is there a person who has never told a lie?

It's completely okay to lie to protect yourself from someone who unjustly wants to hurt you, and it's usually okay to lie when what you're lying about won't hurt anyone anyway.

If you're going to lie, first get familiar with the mechanics, risks, and consequences of lies and lying. Play with lies consciously. Try these lying games out for size:

> Tell a tall tale that could be true.
> Tell a lie that sounds like the truth.
> Pass for something other than what you are.
> Be an imposter at least three different ways.
> Tell a truth that no one will believe.
> Tell two lies that cancel each other out.
> Tell two truths that cancel each other out.

RECOMMENDED: Films: *The Great Imposter, Catch Me If You Can,* and *Big Fish.* Books: *Lying: Moral Choice in Public and Private*

POP QUIZ! All three of these U.S. Presidents got caught lying in office. Who hurt the most people with his lies?

Life by Sissela Bok, *Modern Identity Changer: How to Create and Use a New Identity for Privacy and Personal Freedom* by Sheldon Charrett, and *How to Create a New Identity* by Anonymous.

12. SEND OUT A DISTRESS SIGNAL.

   G

KEYWORDS: hope, faith, self-esteem

Devise a distress signal for yourself to let people know you're in trouble. If you can't say it all directly, say it obliquely.

On the next page are two of about one hundred pen and ink drawings I made in the 1970s, back when I was a member of the Church of Scientology. Scientologists believe that sexual perversion is a sign that a person is evil or in touch with someone else who is evil.

I made these pictures, thinking to myself that someone would see me crying for help. A lot of outlaws and outsiders feel alone and in need of support. Art helps to release such feelings. Draw, paint, or write your distress and let others see it. It doesn't matter if people get it. None of the Scientologists I showed the drawings to

ever did. Or if they did, no one said a word. What mattered to me was that I was drawing these pictures and showing them to people. It helped me to stay alive for years. I knew that eventually someone would get it.

13. ASK FOR HELP.

 ♥♥♥☠   **G**

KEYWORDS: spirit, real life

One of the greatest things about asking for help is that you might actually get some. And still, this can be one of the most difficult alternatives in the book. Even with trusted people in our lives, it may *still* be difficult to do, because for some reason, we often don't feel good about asking for help. But turning to others for comfort and guidance is a necessary part of life. If you've got a friend, lover, or family member you can turn to, do it. If you don't have someone

like that, take a look right now at #47, Find a friend. Keep in mind that people who love you feel *great* when you turn to them for help. So do total strangers. It gives us the opportunity to do something good for someone. Please use this alternative as fre-

quently as you possibly can, because the whole world gets better every time you do.

14. RUN AWAY AND HIDE.

KEYWORDS: safety, real life

Running away and hiding always gives you more options. But it raises some serious questions about courage, honor, and how to get your next meal.

Isn't running away a shameful thing to do? If someone is hurting, abusing, or threatening you, you have every right to run away and hide. You can worry about shame after you've gotten yourself to safety.

What if running away is against my code of honor? There's a flaw in your code of honor. Making peace with ourselves over something we've done is how we teach ourselves not to do dishonorable things in the future. If we need time away in order to make that kind of peace, then we should take that time.

Where do I live and how do I support myself? Buy, borrow, or beg a copy of *The Teenage Liberation Handbook* by Grace Llewellyn. It's a great youth survival guide. Or, visit your friendly neighborhood or online Anarchist bookstore for more age-appropriate books.

What if running away hurts the person I'm running away from or places them in danger? You run. And you make a promise to yourself to try harder not to hurt someone next time.

What if running away hurts an innocent bystander or places an innocent bystander in danger? Well, do they want to go with you? Is it safe to ask them? Take a look at the film *The Great Escape.*

Is there a practice mode? When I was little, I used to run away and hide for periods of ten minutes or so. I doubt my mother ever knew I was doing anything other than playing. Pretend you're hiding away and getting stronger. Does that make you feel better? If so, you can start planning ways to make that happen.

Do I have to leave everyone I love? No. I've hidden out in the open, pretending to be like everyone else. I still do that when I'm feeling fragile. See #27, Give 'em the old razzle-dazzle, and #66, Go stealth.

15. RUN A DIAGNOSTIC PROGRAM.

KEYWORDS: safety, real life

I was once the first mate on a 364-foot motor yacht, which meant it was my job to make sure that the ship would float. A ship, like a person, is in constant motion. The ocean, like the world around us, is in constant motion. And water and salt like to erode pretty much everything they touch.

I used maintenance and diagnostic programs to make sure everything worked and would keep on working. How about developing maintenance and diagnostic programs for the most precious equipment you've got: your mind, body, and spirit? Repairing your life is a lot easier once you've spotted what it is that's broken.

DID SOMETHING TRIGGER YOU? Hungry, angry, lonely, and tired are all feelings that trigger my addictions. Do you have any triggers? Uncock them. Make a list of things that provoke you most and carry it around with you for a while. When you're feeling bad, check the list.

CAN'T STOP YOUR BRAIN? Is everything think, think, think? Balance your mind, spirit, and body. See #2, Take a deep breath and touch yourself.

WHAT'S GOING ON IN YOUR PSYCHIC SPACE? Does your aura need cleansing? Are you under the influence of any jinxes, curses, or prophecies? See #38, Cast a spell. This is a good time to ask for help from spirit guides, angels, familiars, fairies, ghosts, imaginary friends, or God, if you are on speaking terms.

WHAT STATE ARE YOUR HORMONES IN? Puberty, menopause, pregnancy, nursing, and menstrual cycles can affect how you feel, and you can do something to feel better. If you're on any kind of steroids, birth control pills or hormones, and you're having any kind of mood swings, inexplicable weight gain or loss, or changes in body temperature, it'd be worth doing a decent Web search and/or going to see an endocrinologist. Even if you're a guy by birth, this totally applies to you.

CHECK YOUR DOSAGE: If you've slid off any meds, try your best to get back on them to see if that helps. If you think your meds aren't working well or they're causing unwanted side effects, go see the doctor who prescribed them, and if that doesn't help, go see another doctor for a second opinion.

ARE YOU HEARING VOICES? If you are hearing voices and they're telling you to do things that are harmful, go see a psychiatrist. Really. You do not have to obey people or voices that tell you to do bad things. See #6, Just say no.

GET ANOTHER OPINION: Are you unsure of how you're feeling or what to do? Check in with friends who know you well and who treat you kindly and fairly. Or speak up in a twelve-step meeting or to a therapist. This isn't about someone else's ideas being more important than your own. This is just about getting another opinion. See #13, Ask for help.

YOU'D TAKE A PUPPY OR KITTEN TO THE VET IF THEY WERE SICK, RIGHT? Same goes for you. Let me be the good, concerned auntie here. If you have any question about whether or not you should be going to an emergency room or a clinic for a checkup or a check-in, please err on the side of being overly cautious.

HOW ARE YOUR FINANCES? In much debt? Can't pay the bills? Need money to get the fuck out of town but can't seem to raise it? How are you going to pay for your sex change surgery and hormones? Do you have insurance? Have you paid your taxes? There's not much that can make me more scared faster than that litany once it starts in my head. There are ways to deal. See #14, Run away and hide, #13, Ask for help, and #33, Stop fucking around and get to work.

AND ALL THAT JAZZ: Since outlaws don't always have access to traditional Western medicine or religious advice, we're often left on our own to come up with physical and spiritual diagnostic methods that work for us. Here are some other cool diagnostic and maintenance tools you may not have heard about or considered using. Outsider status shouldn't stop you from using these, and some of them are a lot of fun.

Get your aura or chakras cleansed.

Check out kinesiology or use a pendulum to figure out what's good for you and what isn't.

See a homeopathist for a little hair of the dog that bit you.

Read your runes or get a reading.

Read birds' entrails or get a reading. (Okay, not one of the fun ones.)

Get your astrological chart done and check your transits.

Find out if Mercury is in retrograde.

Get or give yourself a Tarot or I Ching reading.

If you're curious, get a fertility or pregnancy test.

Get regular eye and ear checkups. What you see and hear is too important to mess around with.

Get a mammogram or a prostate exam.

See an acupuncturist.

Get tested for allergies.

Get tested for the latest STD, epidemic, or plague. Please.

Give yourself or your lover a breast exam.

16. FIND OUT WHAT YOU LOOK LIKE.

   YG/ASS

KEYWORDS: self-esteem, body, relief

The standards of beauty in America's über-culture are purposefully set too high so that we will buy anything in our frantic scramble to become attractive. We are *meant* to feel crushed, inadequate, and less-than so that we'll buy more and more things in the vain hope of "fixing" ourselves. To combat total self-deprecation, try looking at yourself square in the mirror and taking a fearless inventory of what you see.

> This is a terrifying alternative to killing yourself, but it is totally kick-ass effective, and it isn't dangerous in the least.

Find something attractive about each part of your body for which you've now got negative feelings. Then, focus on those positive feelings. Be as specific as you can about how each part of your body makes you feel, so that you'll know what to feel *better* than. And be as brutally honest about what you like. Keep in mind how other people have complimented you. Can you at least agree with them? In better understanding your body, you can better appreciate it on its own terms. You can begin to experience and view your body in a healthier, kinder way.

ADVANCED MODE: Do this exercise with a friend you really trust, and help each other feel better about your bodies.

17. MAKE A DEAL WITH THE DEVIL.

   G

KEYWORDS: mind game, comfort

I've dealt with the devil. Many people have. Sometimes we want something so badly that we're willing to compromise hard-learned principles of decency, goodwill, and compassion in order to get it. We borrow power that isn't really ours against our better judgment and the general good of humanity. Usually, what we want is something we consider bad, wrong, or sinful, so even when we get what we ask for, we can't enjoy it much. And then payback time forces us to feed power back to that devilish person or institution. It's true what they say: you'll feel like you've sold your soul.

That said, if it comes down to dealing with the devil or taking your own life, deal with the devil. You can try to outsmart the devil—steal from the bad guys and try not to get caught, that sort of thing. You might get away with it. But the only way I've found to escape with my soul intact is to frame my deal in such a way that I don't profit from it.

RECOMMENDED: The film or comic *Constantine*. Both are great.

18. MAKE 'EM LAUGH.

    G

KEYWORDS: safety, delight, mischief

Making people laugh is an excellent way to deflect violence and insults, and reclaim our own voices. It's smoke and mirrors. It gives you the control to focus audience attention where you want it and explore the parts of your suffering that you find humor in. Like my little bald head here. It has tons of possibilities for comedy. If you don't know any

funny things about yourself, see #90, Believe in your own laughter.

POLITICAL MODE: Join or support the Guerilla Girls, the Radical Cheerleaders, the Sisters of Perpetual Indulgence, the Bread and Puppet Theater, and anyone else who's using the comedy of their own lives to undermine America's oppressive über-culture and to restore laughter to our politics and spiritual paths.

ADVANCED MODE: Laugh all the way to the bank. See #34, Sing for your supper.

This alternative to killing yourself is dedicated with love, awe, and respect to Prof. John Emigh, a smart and funny guy indeed.

19. MAKE ART OUT OF IT.

G

KEYWORDS: real life, spirit, mischief

Artistic genius is usually not the product of a life easily lived. The good news about suicidal longing is that it's got the potential to fuel great art. The better news is that whatever has got you thinking about killing yourself will lose its power when you use it to make art instead. The *best* news is that you don't have to be an artist for this alternative to work. Everyone, I repeat, *everyone*, can make art that speaks to someone.

Use any art form that's handy. Write it down, film it, sculpt it, paint it, or set it down in code. You don't have to pay attention to who may or may not look at it. Make art because it's better than being mean and/or hurting anyone, including yourself.

ADVANCED MODE: Some amazing art has been made in service to different communities, causes, or institutions. See #58, Serve somebody, and make some art in service to someone else.

OPTIONAL NEXT STEP: See #20, Sell the stuff you make, and #34, Sing for your supper.

RECOMMENDED: *Art & Fear* by David Bayles and Ted Orland, and *The Artist's Way: A Spiritual Path to Higher Creativity* by Julia Cameron.

20. SELL THE STUFF YOU MAKE.

   G

KEYWORDS: empowering, real life

Stuff tends to sell when it's made from a completely different perspective than most people are used to. Art and craft have value because they can make people think and feel things that they aren't used to thinking or feeling. The truer you are to yourself while you are making your stuff, the more success you'll find in selling it.

Somewhere out there, there's an audience or customer or client or buyer who will pay you for the stuff you make. You can do it. It's tricky, but it is not impossible. There's a network out in the world made up of artists, craftspeople, designers, pornographers, zinesters, adult entertainers, filmmakers, sex workers, *Star Trek* authors, producers, publishers, performers, dealers, sculptors, strippers, writers of horror stories, and *someone* who's already making the sort of art or craft you'd like to be making for a living. People who make stuff tend to overlap and know each other, and we don't tend to be overly competitive. It's been my experience that outlaws are fairly generous in sharing leads and contacts for agents, galleries, producers, presenters, promoters, editors, ghosters, johns, directors, and so on.

The outlaw market doesn't work like the stock exchange, or the mall. To make things run smoothly, you buy stuff directly from the maker and pay cash when you can. You pay fair prices and try not to haggle with artists or hookers. You buy union made. You always tip as big as you can, including street performers. You subscribe to an odd little theater, circus, or orchestra. You eat in your local lesbo veggie restaurant. And as much as you may love Amazon.com, you buy what you can from socialist, anarchist, feminist and independent bookstores. You shop craft fairs, thrift shops, and flea markets. You read locally written porn and erotica. You boycott Wal-Mart. And you do that enough, and gradually, your own work becomes easier and easier to sell for better and better prices. That's how it seems to work.

RECOMMENDED: *Art & Fear* by David Bayles and Ted Orland, anything by Lynda Barry, and any of Alison Bechdel's *Dykes to Watch Out For* series.

21. DEAL WITH THE DEAD AND GONE.

   G/ASS

KEYWORD: comfort

You have every right to deal with the dead and gone any way you want to. When you don't deal with them, they tend to hang around and, for better or for worse, continue to influence your life.

My mother's death left me grieving the hardest. I'd relied so heavily on the near unconditional love we had for each other that her absence made my life extremely difficult to navigate. Without her, I felt alone, abandoned, and unable to continue. In order to come to some peace with my loss, I listed the qualities about my mom that I most admired and relied upon. Then one by one, I embodied those qualities. This helped me to move on.

But it's not always our great loves that die and go. Sometimes, it's the people who made us most afraid. In that case, it would be good to make a list of all the qualities about them we don't admire or rely on, and one by one make sure we're not embodying these things ourselves. Here are some ways you can connect with the dead and gone and come to some final terms with them:

> Get drunk or stoned in their honor and let them walk (not drive) you home.
> Get therapy.
> Talk with them.
> Say a prayer for their well-being.
> Make art out of their lives.
> Light a candle or an everlasting light.
> Dance and/or spit on their grave.
> Play their favorite music.
> Put together a photo collage or album.
> Wear bright red to the funeral.
> Locate them in their next incarnation.

RECOMMENDED: *How to Survive the Loss of a Love* by Melba Colgrove, Ph.D., Harold H. Bloomfield, M.D., and Peter McWilliams. I've gone through dozens of copies.

22. MOISTURIZE!

♥♥♥♥ ☂ ☂ ☂ ☂ **G**
KEYWORDS: comfort, delight, body

Just do it. I am so not kidding about this one.

Femmes, fags, and girly girls know what I'm talking about. *Queer Eye for the Straight Guy* made it okay for boys, men, and butches to moisturize. If you ask nicely, maybe a girly girl or girly boy will show you how to do it.

GREAT CHEAP AND NATURAL MOISTURIZER

2 tablespoons of Aloe Vera gel
3 ounces of olive oil*
1 ounce of cocoa butter
2 ounces of rose water

*For normal skin, use almond or jojoba oil; for dry skin, use sesame oil or lanolin; for oily to blemished skin, use jojoba oil; for mature skin, use rice bran oil or ghee.

To prepare, warm the oil and butter together and the rose water and aloe vera separately. Place all of the ingredients in a blender and whip. If you wish, add scented oils for nice smells. See www.ayurveda.com.

ADVANCED MODE: Moisturize with playmates.

23. SEE YOURSELF IN EVERYONE YOU MEET.

KEYWORDS: delight, rehearsal

G

Will Rogers was an American cowboy humorist, the Garrison Keillor, Jon Stewart, and Ellen Degeneres of his day, all rolled into one sweet, funny guy. He's best remembered for having said, "I never met a man I didn't like." (People talked like that back then. My guess is he probably liked all the women he met, too.) The point is that Will Rogers met a lot of people from all over the world and all walks of life. He met presidents and senators and beauty queens, and he met cowboys and ranch hands and field-workers and freed slaves. And he still said, "I never met a man I didn't like."

By all reports, he was a genuinely nice guy, and he really meant it. Dang! How did he do that? Didn't he ever meet someone who was simply a jerk? Wasn't Will ever in a bad mood? I've been chewing on this one ever since I was a teenager, and I think I figured out how he did it. He must have been a good listener. Good enough to listen to someone so intently that he could always find something they both agreed on, something they had in common. And he must have asked some really good questions to get people to open up to him; he must have shown genuine interest in what they had to say.

The odds are skyrocket high that you've got something in common with anyone you meet, if you listen sincerely enough.

DEBUG MODE: What if you see yourself in someone else and you don't like what you see? Excellent, grasshopper! Use #51, Be your own evil twin, and #91, Believe in your own paradox.

CUT-TO-THE-CHASE MODE: There's a Native American saying that goes something like, "Show me who you love, and I'll know who you are." If you want to get to the heart of a person you're trying to get to know, find out who or what it is they love. Let someone know who or what you love, too.

24. SAVE THE WHALES, THE CHILDREN, OR THE WORLD.

KEYWORDS: comfort, purpose

Choose a charitable or social activist organization. It can be a soup kitchen or human rights group. It can be an animal rights or eco-activism group—any big cause you've always wanted to do something about, or that you never gave much thought to but could certainly get behind. Tell them you'd like to volunteer on a regular basis for one month or one year. At the end of that time, evaluate what you've done and how you feel. Did you feel supported? Were you getting enough of a good feeling from doing that work to make it worthwhile being there? Would you like to leave? Stay another year? You get to choose.

On the other hand, you could try saving one whale, one child, or one tiny little piece of the world. That kind of work is like falling in love or talking with God. If you spend your life that way, always allotting some time to helping out someone else, you shouldn't really need this book much longer.

RECOMMENDED: *Utne Magazine* is a good gateway into the world of worthy causes. As is their website, www.utnereader.com.

25. EXPERIMENT ON ANIMALS AND SMALL CHILDREN.

   YG

KEYWORDS: delight, rehearsal, body

Do you feel awkward about how to deal with other people? Kids and animals respond so well to love and kindness that it's a complete joy to practice your people skills on them. Gizmo is one of the cats I live with. He's more feral than tame. I spend a lot of time learning his rhythms and his boundaries. He spends a lot more time in my lap now, and I pet him using the resilient edge of resistance (see #2, Take a deep breath and touch yourself). If my attention wanders away from him, onto the computer screen or toward someone else in the room, my touch becomes less conscious, and he'll immediately jump down from my lap. He's a high maintenance diva is what he is. But whenever I get cranky, I practice being sweet to him, and it brightens my day. So, give it a try. If you've got no pets or children in your life, you could house-sit, pet-sit, or babysit for friends and family.

Here's a list of basic people skills. Experiment getting these concepts across to animals or children. Practice makes perfect.

Hello.
I'm not going to hurt you.
May I join you?
Thank you.
Where are your boundaries?
Here are my boundaries.
What pleases you?
This is what pleases me.
I enjoyed this time with you.
Good-bye.

26. JOIN A GROUP THAT WANTS YOU AS A MEMBER, OR START YOUR OWN GROUP.

KEYWORD: comfort

We join groups for lots of reasons. Membership keeps us from getting lonely. Maybe a group facilitates some passion of ours. Or, supports us through crises, recovery from addiction, or illness. Some groups have a welcome wagon and an insurance plan.

When you're a freak, a teen, or a recognizable outlaw, you need to search for a group that would have you as a member pretty much just the way you are.

GROUPS YOU COULD JOIN OR START THAT MIGHT WANT EVEN *YOU* AS A MEMBER!

A twelve-step program
A religion
A gang
The Party
A fan club
A union
A garden club
A Macintosh User Group (MUG)
A PC User Group (PUG)
The mile-high club
A guerilla theater group
A culture jamming group
A weekly poker game
A million-$-sales club
A neighborhood association
A local arts, writers, poets, or performing arts group
A glee club or choir
A health club
A book club
A sex club
A dance group
An auto club
A support group
A bereavement support group
An orchestra or band
The polar bear club
A nature club (flora and fauna)
A naturist club (nudists)
A political campaign (yours or someone else's)
A think tank
A volunteer fire department
A convent or monastery
An environmental group
A community center or shelter

WHAT IF THERE'S SOMETHING ABOUT YOU THAT DISQUALIFIES YOU FROM JOINING A GROUP YOU'D REALLY LIKE TO BELONG TO?

Sometimes we join a group because we are hiding who and what we really are while we're learning how to be the person we want to become. That's fine. We all need some time out of the spotlight, with some space to grow and learn. The balancing act is how to maintain your integrity and be worthy of the trust the group is giving you. See #66, Go stealth.

27. GIVE 'EM THE OLD RAZZLE DAZZLE.

KEYWORDS: safety, magic, mischief

Witches and wizards call it glamour. It's not about what you're wearing. It's sweeping someone off their feet by being really attentive. It's sleight of hand, smoke and mirrors, and misdirection. Sometimes, it's a good thing to do when you're scared or uncertain.

You can use glamour as an alternative to living a life of unpopularity and/or loneliness. Razzle dazzle is as effective as you are good at it, and it's a lot easier than you think to get good at. But that's not necessarily good news. Once you're good at glamour, it can become more than a teeny bit addictive. You could start to believe your own mask in order to justify wearing it. You could get pretty smug about yourself, and that's no fun for anyone. Try to keep glamour and razzle dazzle as a tool you use in emergencies or for celebrations.

ADVANCED MODE: Add sexy. You know how you can turn your headlights on someone? Completely make them the center of every single bit of your attention, even without seeming to. It's a talent you can learn just like any other. What do you get from giving 'em a sexy razzle dazzle? Well, what would you *like*? You can add expectations into the mix by being clear and up-front about what you'd like in return for the razzle dazzle you'll be giving. Negotiating an evening like that can be great fun.

HAVE-A-NICER-DAY MODE: Spend a day strolling about, being nothing but perfectly dazzling. Daze and dizzy 'em. Do it solo, or even better, do it with a partner or partners. Call it performance art and charge admission.

28. GIVE YOURSELF PERMISSION.

KEYWORDS: empowering, real life, spirit

Accepting that it's you who must decide what's right and what's wrong for yourself is key to living a fulfilled life. Once you arrive at that conclusion, you don't need permission from anyone else to be or do whatever you want.

Sure, go ahead and get advice from people who've had more experience than you. It also helps to look for advice from people who have a different point of view and to study the rules, regulations, and consequences of doing whatever it is you think you need permission for. But ultimately, it's up to you.

29. PLAY A GAME YOU LIKE TO PLAY.

KEYWORDS: clean slate, delight

Real life isn't like gym class, or some corporate office. Every day you wake up, you get to choose the kind of game you'd like to play and you get to pick what level you'd like to play at. If you don't like a game that someone else wants you to play, you don't have to play it, no matter what anyone says.

SOME GAMES YOU NEVER HAVE TO PLAY:

Corporate America: You don't need an MBA, you never have to dress for success, and you don't have to work for anyone who exploits their workers.

Hail to the Chief: You don't have to support a despot just because he's holding the office of president of the United States.

Monogamy: There's no reason you can't love a lot of people all at the same time.

Saints or Sinners: Sinners get thrown into Hell, and saints lead a really boring life. Totally not a game worth playing.

Don't Ever Tell Anyone What I Did to You: You never have to cover up for anything bad that someone else has done. If someone is asking you to do that, see #14, Run away and hide, and #35, Dance for your life.

30. GET OUT THERE AND BE A STAR!

   YG-50

KEYWORDS: thrill ride

Oh, go for it. At best, you'll be the star you always hoped you could be, and at worst, the journey you're going to take in order to get there will have made your life worth living and wouldn't that be a great feeling?

Every one of us gets to be a star in our own part of the sky. The trick to enjoying the pursuit of stardom is simply to brighten, warm and serve the universe around you. On good days I remember to believe that, and so can you. So, if going for stardom is going to fire up your lust for life, get out there and be a star in whatever sky welcomes you. See #58, Serve somebody.

RECOMMENDED: The films *A Star Is Born* (Judy Garland), *Waiting for Guffman, Yankee Doodle Dandy, Chariots of Fire, Wee Geordie* and *Cabaret*, as well as the book *Edie* by Jean Stein and George Plimpton, and "The Golden Boy," *Worlds' End*, volume 8 of Neil Gaiman's *Sandman* series.

31. GET OUT THERE AND BE AN EXTRA!

   G

KEYWORDS: delight, real life, comfort

Wouldn't it be fun to be one of the background cops or whores on TV's *Law and Order*? Well, move to New York and audition.

Sometimes, it's a lot easier to let someone else be the star of the film.

Extras rarely get lines or credit. Sometimes all the audience ever sees is the back of their head. Or their face on a mug shot in the hand of some TV detective. But you get paid for that, which is a great big plus to being an extra. The trick to personal fulfillment as an extra is understanding that this is your work, that you're dedicating your life to it, and that, by gosh, you're making your living doing it. Life doesn't get much better than that.

32. GET OUT THERE AND BE AN EX.

KEYWORDS: empowering, purpose

What do ex-convicts, transsexuals, ex-nuns, ex-smokers, recovering alcoholics, ex-gamblers, ex-sex addicts, ex-sex offenders, ex-sex workers, and ex-gays have in common with everyone who ever once was but is no longer extremely rich, poor, fat, ugly, beautiful, working class, or ruling class? These are all people who are better known for what they used to be than for what they currently are. That hurts, and I'm sorry if that's happening to you. It seems to be the plight of the postmodern identity that modernist thinkers won't let us freely identity shift. Modernist and fundamentalist logic runs like this: if you once were one of those, then you still are, and you've probably got all those same qualities now. Being an ex is about leaving an old identity behind you, and learning how to manage the stigma of what you once were at the same time. It helps to have someone to talk with who knows what's going on. See #47, Find a friend.

If you're having trouble dealing with someone who refuses to see you as you are today and that situation isn't changing, then see #37, Keep moving on, or if you're feeling more cranky or mischievous, try #52, Be a more frightening monster than the one they think you are. When you embrace being an ex, you can keep or keep available whatever you enjoyed about your past identity. See #7, Trash your preference files and reboot.

MERIT BADGE! Write an essay, poem, song or rant, or make a film, painting or sculpture that responds to the following two questions and you'll be qualified to copy and use this hand-designed-by-me *Ex and Proud Merit Badge*. Heck, you can even earn the right to wear this beauty by meditating on these questions for ten minutes every morning for one week.

1. What do the identities listed at the top of this section have in common?
2. What do you have in common with each one?

ADVANCED MODE: You can use your ex status to get yourself some fame or notoriety, or you can make art out of it. See #30, Get out there and be a star! and #19, Make art out of it.

RECOMMENDED: *Becoming an Ex: The Process of Role Exit* by Helen Rose Fuchs Ebaugh.

33. STOP FUCKING AROUND AND GET TO WORK.

KEYWORDS: real life, empowering

Does it suck being you? Is there nothing worthwhile to do? Does the world owe you a better life than the one you've got? If I said, "Oh, poor you," could you smile?

Say you had a friend, and every day this friend was feeling sorrier and sorrier for herself, so much so that it was hard to spend time with her. Wouldn't you want to tell her enough is enough? If hearing that makes you wince, maybe it's time to get off your butt. Get back to doing something, anything, any kind of work you can find for yourself. You can always keep looking for a more rewarding job. In the summer of 1968, I sorted bottle returns at a Pepsi plant, drove an ice cream truck, and became a scene designer/painter

and a singer/dancer. It was a great summer. I didn't have time to get depressed.

PARTNER MODE: Find a good friend, family member, therapist, twelve-step program, congregation, or coven to help kick your butt back into the world.

RECOMMENDED: Richard Nelson Bolles's *What Color Is Your Parachute?* There's a new edition for teens.

34. SING FOR YOUR SUPPER.

KEYWORDS: real life, spirit, purpose

Are you just too freaky for McDonald's, Disney, or Bank of America? Trust me, that's *good* news. And don't worry about making a living. You can cultivate what makes you freaky to make a much more fun living than what you might find flipping Double-meat burgers, or following some corporate dress code because you think it's your only choice.

Here are just some of the ways I've seen some pretty freaky people make a living without having to hide their freakiness. I've starred the ones I've done myself. This should jumpstart your inner breadwinner.

Accounting, bookkeeping, artists' model,* pelvic model, motion-capture model, astrologer, Tarot reader,* tech support rep,* blogger, zinester, journalist,* bookstore worker, librarian, museum worker, care giver, social worker, sitter,* companion, courtesan, personal assistant, carpenter, cabinetmaker, baker, musician, adult entertainer,* circus, freak show, or sideshow performer, corset maker, craft maker,* game designer, programmer, gardener, landscaper, entertainer,* erotic dancer, sex worker,* stage carpenter,* stage electrician, scene painter,* costumer, sound technician, light technician, stage manager, barista, food-service worker,* restaurant worker, nurse, veterinarian, phone sex operator,* professional dominatrix* or submissive, black-market operator, professional student, pool player, gambler, priest, priestess, nun, minister,* scientist, mathematician, physicist, engineer, boxer, wrestler, grant writer,* grant receiver,* trades and service industry,* U.S. postal worker, theatrical producer or presenter,* artists' agent, slam poet, street/park performer,* sales,* telemarketer,* knitter, tailor, fabric designer, sugar baby.

GROUP MODE: Join or put together a band, writers' group, dance team, theater company, bookstore collective, or socialist commune. AND there are foundations, trusts, grants, and even a few government-sponsored programs that you qualify for precisely because you're an outsider. Get your application in now!

35. DANCE FOR YOUR LIFE.

KEYWORD: safety

The ultimate bully threat is this: entertain me or die. In the Westerns I watched when I was growing up, there was always a scene with some bad guy shooting bullets at the feet of some hapless stranger. And the bad guy would always shout, "Dance! Dance for your life!" Martin Scorsese recreated the moment in *Goodfellas*. The language is grittier. Joe Pesci shouts, "Dance, ya muthahfuckah! Dance!"

Despite romantic notions to the contrary, outlaws and outcasts mostly end up on the wrong side of the gun, both figuratively and literally. Sometimes we have to dance. Sometimes it's someone we love whose finger is on the trigger.

Several of the alternatives in this book will help you get through a bad time like this. You can use #2, Take a deep breath and touch yourself; #6, Just say no; #12, Send out a distress signal; and #14, Run away and hide. I am so sorry if that's the position you're in. If you possibly can, leave now and get to a shelter or even the police. But if you can't leave, keep on dancing for as long as it takes to get out of there and get to someone who can protect you and keep you safe.

36. KILL EVERY LAST ONE OF THOSE MOTHERFUCKERS. (OKAY, NOT REALLY.)

KEYWORDS: thrill ride, relief, mind game

Have you ever had a murderous thought about someone? I have. A lot of people have. I'm sorry, but the kind of world we've all grown up in makes it easy to have those thoughts. So, get over the notion that having them makes you an unusual or bad person. The urge to kill is completely natural. Like any other natural urge, what matters is learning all the constructive things you can do with that urge once it surfaces. Eventually, the urge to kill can channel your energy into a great number of constructive directions. It can fuel your politics, your art, and your sense of justice.

The challenge becomes how can you fully experience and satisfy your urge to kill 'em all without actually killing anyone or anything. The easiest thing to do is pretend you're killing 'em all. Indulge in the revenge fantasies of movies, books, cartoons, and video games.

And when you're ready to come back to the real world, where you know that murder just doesn't cut it, you can decompress the way I did while I was writing this book. I pulled up the San Diego Zoo panda-cam, and I watched Bai Yun in the birthing den with her new cub. Calmed me right down every time.

EROTIC MODE: Hentai is the porn version of manga and anime. If you enjoy playing with violent sex consensually with others, you might want to check it out. Hentai can also be really tender and sweet.

RECOMMENDED: The films *Kill Bill I* and *II*, *Natural Born Killers*, *True Romance*, *Blue Velvet*, *V for Vendetta*, and HBO's *The Sopranos*. *Buffy the Vampire Slayer* solves the problem of violence with good fashion sense. Sword, sorcery, and samurai films can provide you with some really good scenes of death to the bad guys.

37. KEEP MOVING ON.

   G

KEYWORDS: mind game, comfort

Everything comes to an end. What no one ever tells you is what to do after that. This is what you do: you move on and you *keep* moving on. It's not as bad as it sounds.

Moving on is the other side of the mountain from death and dying. It's about what you do after the dying and after the death. It's wherever life takes you after the end of something that was beautiful and important or ugly and painful in your life.

> There's an old saying in show business: all shows close.

Moving on is what you do after a relationship is over, whether it was a relationship with someone, something, or someplace. Moving on is about continuing your life without that physical presence.

You choose to move on when you stop falling back into an identity that no longer works for you.

It's a way you can start all over again and put all the painful or joyful good-byes in context with the hellos that always follow. How can you tell when something is over? I'm still learning that one, but usually I get the message when I feel stuck or when I'm in too much pain, and good-bye is one of the very few options left. Sure, moving on can leave you bone lonely, but most of that loneliness happens when you're lost in memories. Part of moving on successfully is learning what to leave behind. See #21, Deal with the dead and gone, and #100, Tidy your campsite before you leave.

Make a list of the last three people, places, or things that you lost or left behind. Which parts of you haven't moved on from those losses? See #9, Make longer-range plans, and figure out how best to move on from those losses.

RECOMMENDED: Try the books *Berlin Stories* by Christopher Isherwood, *Breakfast at Tiffany's* by Truman Capote, and *Siddhartha* by Hermann Hesse. Or rewatch any season finale of the TV show *Buffy The Vampire Slayer* by Joss Whedon.

38. CAST A SPELL.

♥♥ ☠ ☠   ↑ ↑ ↑   G

KEYWORDS: magic, safety

Are you good at making things happen across the room or across time? Do you travel interdimensionally or would you like to? Do you have your own version of spider sense or women's intuition? Are you a medium or a teller of fortunes? Are you worried that someone is going to dump pig's blood on you at the prom?

You are not alone, and you are not freaky or crazy for any supernatural abilities you seem to have. There's a whole world of people who practice all kinds of magic. There are books, audio and video tapes, and DVDs on how to do it. There are conventions of people who practice real live cast-a-spell magic. Some of them, but not many, worship Satan. Even so, almost all of these people are very nice to hang out with and learn magic from. Part of the fun is looking for these people in your life. So, go learn some magic and have fun casting spells. Don't poke your eye out with your wand.

SEX MAGIC MODE: Throw in an orgasm to fuel your magic. It's fun and easy! Read *Urban Tantra: Sacred Sex for the 21st Century* by my partner in love, art, and magic, Barbara Carrellas.

39. MAKE A WISH.

    G

KEYWORDS: spirit, magic, purpose

When you wish upon a star, your dreams come true. Did you ever believe that? What made you stop believing? When was the last time you made a wish on a wishbone, a dandelion, or a birthday candle? If making wishes makes you feel better, make more wishes. I mean, duh!

Think of something you'd like. Anything at all. Now, savor the idea of already having it. How does that make you feel? For the rest of the day, do things that make you feel just like that.

What you're doing is putting yourself in a receptive mode so that your wish might come true. You're aligning yourself with the naturally positive energy of the universe that wants you to be happy.

40. MAKE BELIEVE.

KEYWORDS: comfort, purpose, rehearsal

When you make believe, you're giving yourself clues to a useful future identity.

Beyond the age of eight or nine, very few people take make-believe seriously. Pretending is a skill we spend years perfecting, and yet we're never supposed to use that skill for any real purpose. You, however, can take this skill very seriously and use it to make yourself feel better.

Making believe isn't exactly lying, and it's not a way to "fake it 'til you make it," because when you make believe, it's as real as you can imagine it to be. And making believe isn't delusional, it's completely conscious. How many real-life uses can you come up with for your skill in making believe?

EXERCISE: Make believe you're somehow better than you are right now. Or, make believe you're the kind of you that you've always wanted to be. Use costumes, props, and as many details as you might need to help you make believe that you are that better you. Keep on making believe for as long as you can. Then write down the differences between the make-believe you and the everyday you. Use #7, Trash your preference files and reboot, or #38, Cast a spell, to get rid of the parts of you that make you feel bad, and nurture the parts of you that make you feel better about yourself.

RECOMMENDED: *Calvin and Hobbes, The Secret Life of Walter Mitty* (movie and book), and *Tipping the Velvet* (movie and book).

WOO-WOO MODE: #49, Find a God who believes in you.

41. MAKE A DREAM COME TRUE FOR SOMEONE ELSE.

   G

KEYWORDS: delight, purpose

It's been said that the dining rooms in Heaven and Hell are exactly the same. Diners sit across from each other at long tables heaped with delicious food. The only utensils are three-foot-long chopsticks. In Hell, the damned starve as they try in vain to feed themselves with the chopsticks that can't reach their mouths. In Heaven, folks generously feed one another across the table. Making someone else's dreams come true makes you feel great. It doesn't have to be their dream of a lifetime. Leave that to reality TV. Just go make someone's little dream come true with no strings attached.

If this is you with the wings, whose shoulder might you be sitting on?

RECOMMENDED: See the film *Pay It Forward* and visit the Pay It Forward Foundation at www.payitforwardfoundation.org/.

42. ACT YOUR AGE OR ANY OTHER.

KEYWORDS: real life, empowering, mischief

Age-based discrimination is a given. But here's a way you can get around it. No matter how old you are, you can embody an archetype of *any* age and live at the age that works best for you at any given moment. Most cultures have established archetypes for what they determine to be the four primary ages of life. These are represented in the Tarot as King (elder), Queen (adult), Knight (adolescent), and Page (child). And while those are nice enough categories, they're too broadly drawn to be of much practical use.

As an outsider in a postmodern age, you're free to try out many nuanced identities within, and beyond, each of those four age ranges. You can take on and put off ages as they suit you, using different age models to handle different situations in your life. You can shift identities in order to stay under the radar of someone who isn't hip to what you're doing.

Here's a list of identities I've used that you can pull out of your hat whenever you need it. You can be each and every one of them. Have a great time.

CHILDREN
The Good Kid
The Girly Girl
The Tomboy
The Nerd
The Invisible Kid

ADOLESCENTS
The Romantic
The Rebel
The Freak
The Slut
The Sex Genius
The Dyke
The Goth
The Slayer

ADULTS
Mother/Mommy
Father/Daddy
The Scientist
The Nun/Monk
The Leader
The Teacher
The Whore
The Outlaw
The Owner

ELDERS
Grandma
Grandpa
The Crone
The Ambassador
The Curmudgeon
The Judge
The Wizard

AGELESS
The Lady
The Gentleman
The Artist
The Lunatic
The Magician
The Traveler
The Healer
The Monster
The Student

43. ACT YOUR GENDER OR ANY OTHER.

   YG-50

KEYWORDS: comfort, delight, empowering

More and more people are embracing multiple genders in order to accomplish things in different parts of their lives. Sometimes, we need boy energy. Sometimes, only girly-girl energy will do. You get to do what you most enjoy doing, no matter what your body looks like, or what gender you were assigned at birth. When did you learn otherwise?

Growing up in our culture, we learn to narrow down our gender presentation to the same one every day. If you were raised in another culture, your gendered behavior would look very different from the way you're doing your gender right now. It would follow that we have the ability to be lots of genders. But there's never been a practical guideline for shifting between them. Well, there is now. Welcome to g.i.d.g.e.t., the gender identity graphic equalizer tool. You can use g.i.d.g.e.t. to pinpoint both the gender you are being, and the gender you'd like to be. It's easy as pie and it doesn't involve surgery or hormones. Woo-hoo!

Why play with gender? If gender is an identity that signals our desire and our position in some power hierarchy, then it should be possible to explore the nature of our desire and power more completely by taking on a gender identity more compatible with our fantasies. Wouldn't that be a good reason to stay alive?

Take a look at the chart on the next page. Each column represents a binary pair of characteristics. Make an X in each column to indicate more or less where you tend to fall most of the time. Modify any words you like. Use the blank column to add any other qualities that help define who you most usually are being. When you're done, connect the X's with a line. Voila! It's a graphic representation of the gender you spend a lot of your day-to-day time in.

Now, get yourself to a nice, safe, comfortable place where you can be by yourself with as little chance of being interrupted as possible. Think of something that turns you on sexually. Just close your eyes and imagine doing it or having it done to you. What does it make you feel like? Write down some words. Take your time and be thorough in your imagination.

Once you've got a sexual fantasy in mind, go back to g.i.d.g.e.t. and enter a check mark in each column that would most closely represent *how you feel when you imagine it*. Then connect the check marks with a line that's different from the one you first made. Now you know the components of a gender identity that most closely matches the gender in which you experience your sexual fantasy. And being the clever thing that you are, you can now consciously adjust yourself along several binaries in order to give yourself pleasure. It's that easy. That's how sexual fantasies can lead to personal enlightenment and freedom—even your grossest, most scary, don't-wanna-go-there sexual fantasies.

REMEMBER: You don't ever have to act out on your own fantasies, or anyone else's. Ever. It's always your choice.

Gender Identity Graphic Equalizer Tool

Leader	Orderly	Insider	Adult	Gallant	Mind	Solid	Light	Reason	Anything Else?
+3	+3	+3	+3	+3	+3	+3	+3	+3	+3
+2	+2	+2	+2	+2	+2	+2	+2	+2	+2
+1	+1	+1	+1	+1	+1	+1	+1	+1	+1
0	0	0	0	0	0	0	0	0	0
-1	-1	-1	-1	-1	-1	-1	-1	-1	-1
-2	-2	-2	-2	-2	-2	-2	-2	-2	-2
-3	-3	-3	-3	-3	-3	-3	-3	-3	-3
-3	-3	-3	-3	-3	-3	-3	-3	-3	-3
Follower	Chaotic	Outsider	Child	Gracious	Body	Fluid	Dark	Passion	Anything Else?

POWER MODE: Now that you've run g.i.d.g.e.t. to explore your desire, run it to explore the nature of your power. What points within the binaries make you feel powerful? How could you become the kind of identity who more routinely feels powerful?

ZEN MODE: Zero yourself out in every column of g.i.d.g.e.t.

44. USE THE WRONG TOOL FOR THE JOB.

   YG/ASS

KEYWORDS: real life, mischief

The master's tools will never dismantle the master's house.
—Audre Lorde

So what tools could you use? The wrong ones! You can get really good at using the wrong tools to get the job done.

Most outsiders and outcasts have been on the receiving end of a bully's anger, so we are nearly always at first loathe to use a bully's methods. But after a while and usually under a great deal of pressure, some of us embrace those tools and turn them on our oppressors. I know a lot of people swear by that, but I'm trying my best not to use the following tools:

Force	Threats
Power over	Humiliation
Shame	Blame
Fear	Name-calling
Hate	Segregation
Black-and-white thinking	Capitalism
The notion that the end justifies the means	Divide and conquer
Intimidation	Theft
An eye-for-an-eye	Greed

When you don't use the master's tools, other tools become available to you. These aren't startling new tools. Most of them have been in use for aeons. They're the tools the bullies have tossed aside as forbidden or unworkable because they're too scared to use them.

Magic	Compassion
Love	Humor
Anarchy	Comedy
Sex	Paradox
Joy	Nonviolence
Patience	Seduction
Fairness	Riddles
Consensus	Art
Illogic	Visualization
Compromise	Affirmations
Culture jamming	

EXERCISE: Add more items to both lists of tools.

PRACTICE MODE: Do something nice for the wrong reason.

ARTSY MODE: Make art from the wrong materials.

WOO-WOO MODE: Worship God the wrong way.

MATH MODE: Solve a problem using the wrong formula.

SEX MODE: Find a fun sex toy at your local bakery.

ALTERNATE SEX MODE: Find a fun sex toy at the hardware store.

HEAVY METAL SEX MODE: Find a fun sex toy in a medical catalog.

TRANNY MODE: Do it the way you did it before you transitioned.

GANDHI MODE: Get together with, or help put together, a group of people who agree on which part of the master's house needs to be dismantled. Reach consensus on how to dismantle it without using any of the master's tools.

45. COME OUT, COME OUT, WHATEVER YOU ARE.

   YG/ASS

KEYWORDS: empowering, delight, purpose

It's always worth the risk to come out of whatever closet we've been keeping ourselves in. But each of us is entitled to make the decision about just how and when to do it.

We keep secrets about ourselves when we're afraid that if someone knew, they would stop loving us and/or start hurting us. While it's true that some people are going to say good-bye, there will be people who are going to say hello, just because you're being a you that you've always wanted to be. And you've seen enough television and movies, and read enough books or graphic novels to know that it takes a lot of work to keep a secret about your identity from those who love you. Keeping a secret, staying in some closet, never expressing some loving part of ourselves can drain our energy to the point of exhaustion. And then there's all the paranoia about someone finding out. It makes you jumpy. So, come on out. You don't have to come out to everyone all at once. Start by coming out to someone that other people have safely come out to.

And remember, just because you come out as something, that doesn't mean you have to always keep on being that. You can always come out as something else later.

46. FIND THE LOVE OF YOUR LIFE.

    G

KEYWORDS: thrill ride, body, delight

I swear, there's someone out there for you to love. He, she, or they are out there someplace looking for you. But no one is going to love you exactly the way you are until *you* love

If you were in this picture,
who would you be?

you exactly the way you are. So, how do you love yourself? Louise Hay says it would be very brave of you if you were to say, "I love you just the way you are" in the mirror three times a day. For more affirmations, see her book *You Can Heal Your Life*.

ZEN MODE: Become the kind of person you want to fall in love with. Make a list of what's important in a lover, and work on being that yourself. See *Be the Person You Want To Find* by Cheri Huber.

47. FIND A FRIEND.

KEYWORDS: real life, comfort safety

You can do it. Finding a friend is like finding anything else. You just keep looking until someone shows up in your life who's genuinely glad to see you. Then, you take a deep breath, open up, and let someone in at whatever level of friendship makes you both comfortable.

> One of the most difficult things about being a recognizable freak or outsider is the loneliness. It's harder to make friends.
>
> One of the *best* things about being a recognizable freak or outsider is that your best friends don't mind, and usually even appreciate, a lot of the weird stuff about you.

No matter who you are or what you do, there are people who would like to spend time with you. Whenever you're feeling lonely, just take a moment to consider how many different friends are really possible in your life. A friend can be a political ally, a classmate, a mentor, or a lover. You can make friends at the library, a potluck, at Good Vibrations or a Toys In Babeland store, or in a twelve-step meeting. Just go do what interests you, and before long you'll be doing that with other people who have the same interests.

PRACTICE MODE: Practice friendship with pets, imaginary friends, dolls, action figures, stuffed animals, and video games. And you *do* have a friend in Jesus, as well as in Mohammed, Moses, Buddha, Joseph Smith, Mary

If you were in this picture, who would you be?

Baker Eddy, L. Ron Hubbard, and any other spiritual guide, angel, or demon who listens and/or speaks to you.

ADVANCED MODE: Try to structure your life so it includes friends from a wide range of your life's experiences, and from a wide diversity of identities.

48. FIND YOUR TRIBE.

KEYWORDS: comfort, relief, safety

Tribes are about family and community. You have every right to the kind of loving parent/child or sibling relationship you've always wanted to have, whether it's in addition to your family of birth or instead of it. No matter how old you are, there are kind souls in the

If you were in this picture, who would you be?

world who'd love to be your daddy, mommy, son, daughter, puppy, kitten, or baby. You could find someone who would be a wonderful big brother or little brother. You could find a big sister or kid sister. You could even find your evil twin, or a couple of kissin' cousins. All these kinds of tribal and familial love exist in the world for you. You just have to go looking.

MEMBERSHIP HAS ITS PRICE: Sometimes we give up some of our individuality in order to be accepted into some tribe or so that we can become the kind of person that someone else wants us to be. It's not a good situation to be in for any length of time. Use #15, Run a diagnostic program, every now and then and #37, Keep moving on, if it comes to that.

49. FIND A GOD WHO BELIEVES IN YOU.

♥♥♥♥   ⬆ ⬆ ⬆ ⬆   G

KEYWORDS: comfort, magic, spirit

Postmodern identities that require deities require postmodern deities. If you're thinking that life isn't worth living in part because God doesn't approve of something that you are or that you're doing, it's time you find yourself a God who likes people like you. Look around. There are perfectly lovely deities who watch over nature, science, and art. There are deities who will support you on pretty much any career path you choose to take. As a postmodern identity surfer, you'll find new Gods and Goddesses to bless each new identity you take on. Do be sure to say a respectful farewell to the Gods and Goddesses you leave behind.

Here are some good questions to ask on your quest for a God who believes in you:

- Is it possible that there are Gods and Goddesses out there besides the one you've been believing in?
- Have you heard of any other Gods or Goddesses who give their followers a better deal at life than your God is giving you?
- Does the culture you live and work in worship a deity or deities who look and act like you?
- Have you heard of any other deities who *do* look and act like you? Have you looked hard?
- Who is your deity or deities, and what are they doing for you right now? In what currency and how much are you paying them for what they do?
- If your world came down to intelligent design, what is the nature of your God's intelligence? Do you want to be intelligent like that?
- Who exactly is the God who's being worshipped by the people who are giving you trouble? How does *their* God want to be worshipped, and what is their God doing for them, do you think, that makes Him worth their worship?

ZEN MODE: Believe in no single creator God, but that anything else is possible.

WICCAN MODE: Believe in Gods and Goddesses in nature, and in elves, faeries and other wee folk when they give you cause or comfort to believe in them.

BIOLOGICAL EVOLUTIONARY MODE: Use wild, wacky sex and gender positive nature as your deity. Read *Evolution's Rainbow: Diversity, Gender and Sexuality in Nature and People* by my smart friend and colleague, Joan Roughgarden.

RECOMMENDED: *Siddhartha* by Hermann Hesse and Jean Shinoda Bolen's *Goddesses in Everywoman* and *Gods in Everyman*. Play *Black & White*, the video game.

50. BE YOUR OWN HERO/INE.

KEYWORDS: delight, empowering, real life

No matter what genre or generation we're talking about, superhero/ines are always outsiders, mutants, and/or freaks. It is their particular superpower that substantiates their freakishness. Their ability to navigate the world in spite of their shocking difference is part of what makes them super.

When the universe took away your respectable identity membership card, it gave you a miraculous gift in exchange: the precise superpowers you need in order to rescue yourself from suffering and keep living in this world. And like all truly great hero/ines, your life's mission, should you choose to accept it, is to discover your own superpowers and then use them to help end suffering for everyone. Start looking for your superpowers right now. You'll find them very close to whatever it is that's keeping you on the outside of things.

51. BE YOUR OWN EVIL TWIN.

KEYWORDS: safety, real life, mischief

If being good isn't helping you handle your life, then be bad. Your evil twin is the perfect identity to call on when you want to break a stupid rule for the first time. The best evil twins on television and in the movies are always braver, sexier, and lots more fun anyway. Cover your bases safetywise, lay down the don't-be-mean ground rule, and then let your evil twin run the show for a while.

ADVANCED MODE: Be you and your evil twin at the same time. See #91, Believe in your own paradox.

52. BECOME A MORE FRIGHTENING MONSTER THAN THE ONE THEY THINK YOU ARE.

KEYWORDS: mischief, delight, magic

If people knew the real you, would they run screaming from the room? Well, whatever kind of monster they *think* you are, it's probably safe to say, you're really much *more* terrifying. Sometimes we like to look freaky. Sometimes we like to blend in. It's our choice. But shifting from one to another keeps people from figuring out who or what we are.

The cultural monster here at the turn of the century is the shape-shifter. Being an out-sider isn't what makes us monstrous. We are monsters because we're so good at either revealing our monstrosity, or keeping it hidden when we want to.

It's when we become something the über-culture can't quite put its finger on that we know we're being a worse monster than the one they think we are. In this culture, that's a crime. You have to match your photo ID. So, go ahead. Be a chameleon. Enjoy yourself. Play safe, and try not to scare the little children.

EXTRA CREDIT: Write an essay, poem, recipe, film or perfor-mance piece on this question: if a culture's monsters reflect it's greatest fears, what does it say about über-American culture that its monsters are for the most part shape-shifters and mutants?

53. BE CUTE OR BE DASHING.

KEYWORDS: delight, empowering, body

When you spend a lot of your time dodging arrows, it's good to have a friendly way to disarm the archers. Cute doesn't mean weak, subservient, or incapable of protecting oneself. To the contrary, cute is distinctively capable of inflicting serious damage. Porcupines are super cute, but you wouldn't want to fuck with one.

Cute and dashing are age-free, race-free, class-free and gender-free identities. You don't need any particular look to be cute or dashing—it's cross-cultural. You don't need to spend money on any particular accessories. Like most things, they work best if you don't force it. So, get on out there and be cute or dashing.

ADVANCED MODE: Be gracious or be gallant.

54. BE AFRAID. BE VERY AFRAID.

KEYWORDS: empowering, clean slate, purpose

Use your fear like a compass. Each time I walk toward what's scaring me most—and keep on walking toward it—I end up walking right through that fear to some other side where I am no longer afraid. And every time *that* happens, there's *another* fear waiting for me on the other side. And I bitch and moan and then start walking toward this new fear, and it always gets scarier and scarier until finally I'm through to yet another side with yet another fear. It's like a video game. The levels get harder and harder, but you get better and better at playing.

RECOMMENDED: *Jonathan Livingston Seagull* by Richard Bach and Albert Brooks's film *Defending Your Life*. (Watch out for Shirley MacLaine's cameo!

55. BE ORGASMICALLY CELIBATE.

     G

KEYWORDS: delight, comfort, body

At some time, everyone needs, or just plain wants, some downtime from sex with other people. For some people, that downtime can last our entire lives. It doesn't mean we're damaged or that we've got a history of sexual abuse, although it could mean either.

Wanting a break from sex with other people doesn't mean you need to do without sex. Sexual energy is healing, comforting, strengthening energy, and sometimes we just need to stoke our own fires. That's a good and natural and even healthy thing to do. You are chock full of yummy sexual energy, and you don't have to share it with anyone.

RECOMMENDED: Start with the classic book *Sex for One: The Joy of Self-Loving* by Betty Dodson. For more resources, visit the websites of Planned Parenthood, Toys in Babeland, and Good Vibrations.

56. GET LAID. PLEASE.

     G

KEYWORDS: delight, comfort, body

There is no legitimate moral, spiritual, or physical reason you shouldn't have some great sex if that's what you want. Keep in mind, however, that there may be legal implications depending on your age and the kind of sex you've got in mind. There are only three rules you need to follow for carefree, guilt-free safer sex of any kind: be consensual, don't be mean, and use safer sex guidelines.

When you follow these rules, you get to toss out any of your older rules about sex. You are chock full of yummy sexual energy, and you can share it safely, sanely, respectfully, and consensually whenever and with whomever you like. I draw the line at sex between children and adults. I don't see *that* one working at all.

HOT SEX TIPS and Dating Advice

FOR YOUNG FOLK

Sex can be right this minute or next year some time. You get to decide. And you get to change your mind about that whenever you want to.

Sex can be a passionless quickie.

Sex can be any way you imagine it can be.

Sex doesn't have to be any way you don't want it to be.

Sex doesn't have to be with one person over a long period of time, or even with one person at a time.

Sex doesn't have to be with anyone but yourself. You get to control the guest list.

Sex doesn't have to happen with anyone of any particular race, religion, gender, age, class, education level or body type.

Sex doesn't have to be for free. You can buy, sell or trade sex for things if you need and want to do that.

Sex doesn't mean you're a slut or a whore, unless of course that's what you'd like to be.

Sex doesn't have to be genital, and you don't have to do it in private.

Sex doesn't have to end with an orgasm for everyone.

During sex, you can be any gender, age, race, class, animal, object, or alien life form that you'd like to be as long as you both or all agree that that's what you're safely and respectfully being together.

Sex doesn't have to be in the missionary position.

Sex doesn't have to happen on a bed in a bedroom in the dark.

Sex can be really yummy, sicko, gross, painful, scary, bloody, and/or degrading when you all or both agree to do it that way safely and respectfully together.

Sex can be hilariously funny.

Sex can be a lovely gift you give someone or someone gives you.

Sex can be a blessing, a prayer, and a generous act of healing.

Sex can involve costumes, props, and a script.

Sex can be as soon as you put down this book or while you're still holding it.

57. SAY PLEASE AND THANK YOU.

KEYWORDS: mischief, thrill ride, delight

Okay, so you're someone who doesn't fit in. That doesn't mean you have to be surly about it. The very best outlaws are the charming ones, anyway. So, be well mannered. Chicks and moms love it, and guys will want to do guy bonding with you. Thank you is a great and easy way to feel better. When anyone gives you a compliment, take a moment to hear it, enjoy it, and say thank you. Try it for a week. See if please and thank you make a difference in your outlaw life.

ADVANCED MODE: Become gracious and be a lady, or become gallant and be a gentleman. See #43, Act your gender or any other.

WAY ADVANCED MODE: Say, "I'm sorry," and ask people to apologize to you.

58. SERVE SOMEBODY.

KEYWORDS: purpose, delight, rehearsal

When I run out of reasons to stay alive for my own sake, it always helps to donate a substantial part of my life to the service of somebody else.

All my life I've wanted to be useful. I've always wanted to help. I've wanted to make people smile or laugh. My two most intense periods of service have been my twelve years of willing and eager service to the Church of Scientology and my ten months of willing and eager sadomasochistic service to two phenomenal dykes. I don't know which makes me look crazier in the eyes of the dominant culture. But I do know that the times of my life I've spent in service have been the happiest times of my life, and I don't regret a minute of it. Giving is a most humbling and rewarding experience, and is a wonderful reason to go on living.

59. EROTICIZE THE PAIN.

KEYWORDS: comfort delight

Sometimes, the only way to deal with pain is to transform it into erotic energy. What's erotic energy? You get to decide, but it's in the general area of yum.

Try doing this: Pinch your arm. While it's still hurting, mentally transform the pain into warmth. Just decide that what you're feeling is warmth and direct that warmth into your heart, where it feels good. Once you can regularly transform pain and direct it to your heart as warmth, start directing your transformed pain to other places in your body. You can direct warm, healing energy to any muscle, bone, or organ you've got. That's all there is to it. This alternative works best when you know and/or you're willing to test your limits.

60. BAKE A CAKE.

♥♥♥♥ ⛱ ⛱ ⛱ ⛱ **G**

KEYWORD: delight

Oh, go ahead. It's fun and easy! You can bake it from scratch or out of a box. You can do it solo or with a friend or family members. You give pieces to people or you could even eat the whole darned thing yourself. The eat-it-all-yourself option works up to a point, and then it becomes something you wanna stop doing. See #61, Eat it all and keep it down, which happens to be next.

61. EAT IT ALL AND KEEP IT DOWN.

♥♥☠☠ ⛱ **G**

KEYWORDS: comfort, if you must

Too much fat on your body can be hard on your heart, your back, and your knees. But sometimes this seems like the only alternative to being miserable. A lot of people go through eating binges. I always have. It's when we know what we're eating isn't good for us and that it's too much to be eating. Often, we even pass the point of enjoying what we're eating, and anxiety about *that* starts to creep in.

It's a stopgap. I wish I could easily stop overeating, but it usually takes me noticing that all my clothes are too tight and that I've put on ten pounds before I start swinging the other way. Try to overeat with friends so that you can slow each other down from time to time.

RECOMMENDED: Overeaters Anonymous didn't work for me. But I am a lifetime member of Weight Watchers, which has given me a realistic, balanced, and thoroughly fulfilling way to eat.

Alternatives to eating that have worked for me are #58, Serve somebody; #15, Run a diagnostic program; and #16, Find out what you look like. As a last resort, there's always #81, Starve yourself.

62. STAY IN BED.

KEYWORD: comfort

You know this works, so go ahead. Don't feel so guilty about it. There always have been, and always will be, days in your life when it's just better to stay in bed. The great news is you get better at giving in to the inevitable, and you stop feeling guilty.

I settle in with a bowl of cream of tomato soup and a box of Cheez-Its, and I watch an entire season of *Buffy* on DVD. Go, rest.

ARE YOU A LAZYBONES? You know what's a reasonable length of time for you to be completely zoned out, so set an alarm and when the alarm goes off, try #33, Stop fucking around and get to work.

ALREADY IN BED? If you're confined to bed, and reality is no place you want to be living in, you can go to Tahiti in your mind, or to any other place you'd like to visit. See #40, Make believe, and #91, Believe in your own paradox.

63. TRAVEL AND HAVE ADVENTURES.

KEYWORDS: empowerment, spirit, thrill ride

 Outlaws and outcasts tend to wander like the lost tribes of Israel, searching for a home—someplace where our bodies, hearts, and souls aren't in thrall to some heartless, soulless über-culture. I travel to evade the grasp of that über-culture and its bullies, and sometimes I travel just for the heck of it. It's how I stay amused by and interested in living an outlaw life.

FIRST-AID MODE: Take a sentimental journey to someplace where you feel better or remember great times.

ZEN MODE: Travel without a destination.

ALTERNATE ZEN MODE: Travel without moving.

WOO-WOO MODE: When a physical journey isn't possible, take a journey along some elemental path of emotions, body, mind, will, and/or spirit. Use Tarot cards to keep track of your travels. The four suits represent the journeys we take through our emotions, the physical world, our mind's growth, and the state of our will. There are four face cards in each suit, usually drawn as kings, queens, knights, and pages. I use the four face cards to represent different ages: elders, adults, adolescents, and children. The Tarot also includes twenty-two major arcana cards, numbered zero to twenty-one, which represent a spiritual journey ranging from complete innocence to complete worldliness.

S P E C I A L   B O N U S   F E A T U R E !

Be the first on your block to build the *Hello, Cruel Tarot Deck*!

Get an old Tarot deck, preferably one with pictures you like. Tape over the words. For the face cards, choose one identity each from the child, adolescent, adult, and elder identities found in #42, Act your age or any other, and write it on the tape you've placed on each face card. For the twenty-two major arcana, you can use the twenty-two outlaw values from #89, Shatter some family values.

The journey of Pentacles, the suit that represents the physical plane, including your body.

1. Opportunity
2. Responsibility
3. Craft
4. Corporation
5. Rage
6. Borders
7. Illusion
8. Waste
9. Peace
10. Generosity

The journey of Swords, the suit that represents your mind, including language.

1. Identity
2. Consequence
3. Hierarchy
4. Culture
5. Fame
6. Purity
7. Struggle
8. Burn out
9. Humiliation
10. Self-sacrifice

The journey of Wands, the suit that represents willpower and intentions.

1. Power
2. Opposition
3. Union
4. Isolation
5. Madness
6. Passage
7. Exchange
8. Good-bye
9. Compromise
10. Empathy

The journey of Cups, the suit that represents emotions and feelings.

1. Hello
2. Question
3. Harmony
4. Family
5. Grief
6. Comfort
7. Excess
8. Risk
9. Fulfillment
10. Delight

Each card is a step on a journey. If you're stuck or lost, try to spot the card closest to where you are. The very next card may well be what you need in order to feel better. Similarly, numbered cards are in harmony with each other, so a card of the same number in another suit may work even better as a next step in your journey.

RECOMMENDED: Any book by the merry mistress of Tarot, my dear friend Rachel Pollack, to whom this alternative is lovingly dedicated.

But wait! What's the use of having a spiritual path if you can't customize it for your own spirit?!

Eventually, your favorite pathways through your emotions, body, mind, will, and spirit will emerge, and you'll replace my words and ideas with your own. And I think that's how the world is supposed to get better and better for each of us having lived in it.

64. GO ON A QUEST.

   G

KEYWORDS: empowering, spirit, purpose

A quest is your agreement to set out on a journey and to keep on going until you meet up with some great Ah-HAH! Go ahead. Nothing's stopping you. If you know what it is you're in search of, just walk out the door and start looking. The odds are good that anything that catches your attention will be some kind of clue. Or, if walking isn't an option, start Web surfing, or get someone to share their favorite books with you. Or, go chase a rabbit down some hole.

If you were in this picture, who would you be?

When you've discovered something, come on back and tell the rest of us.

OPTIONAL PREPATORY STEP: #5, Finish your homework first.

RECOMMENDED: *That Which You Are Seeking Is Causing You to Seek* by Cheri Huber.

65. GO SHOPPING.

KEYWORD: comfort

Going shopping to make yourself feel better doesn't always work, but it's worth a try. You don't have to buy anything; you could just look. But if you get the urge to buy something you can't afford or don't even need or want, take a moment to figure out how buying that and having that would make you

feel. Then take another moment to figure out how to give yourself that same feeling without doing the buying. Sometimes that works for me. See #40, Make believe.

RECOMMENDED: *I Want That!* by Thomas Hine, and *We Know What You Want* by Douglas Rushkoff.

66. GO STEALTH.

KEYWORDS: safety, delight, comfort

YG

Every outlaw, freak, or outsider dreams at one time or another of passing for normal, and not having to deal with the staring and the questions and the laughing and the harassment.

Moments of stealth are moments free from all that. After spending a lot of time looking over your shoulder to see if you're being followed, there's nothing like the wonder and relief of looking at the world through a "normal" pair of eyes.

The trick to managing your personal integrity while going stealth is to work at being the same you, no matter what else you're being. Keep adjusting degrees of stealth in different parts of your life until you wind up with the most opportunities for having a whole lot of harmless fun. It takes time, but it works. See #98, Learn moderation in all things.

RECOMMENDED: T-Gina comics at www.t-gina.com. Artist Gina Kamentsky tackles issues of stealth vs. visible outlaw with delightful good humor and compassion.

67. GO FOR IT AGAINST ALL ODDS.

KEYWORDS: thrill ride, empowering, purpose

Going for it against all odds is one of the cooler things that humans seem to do naturally. It doesn't necessarily mean going for it right now, and it doesn't have to mean putting every bit of your energy into it until you have no more left. Going for it against all odds can simply mean moving forward or standing still with persistence, and understanding that every move you make in your life—no matter what it is—can always be a move in the direction of achieving your dream.

Take inspiration from your favorite mythical, supernatural, or fantastical characters who keep hurling themselves against impossible obstacles and emerging triumphant. Do a thorough Internet search to discover the strategies they use. Let what you find inspire you to use the same tactics to search for an identity you enjoy being that is persistent, brave, or foolish enough to tackle your greatest fears and reach for your greatest dreams.

68. GO COMPLETELY BATTY.

   ASS

KEYWORDS: safety, comfort, if you must

Madness is an unconscious coping mechanism we develop either to compensate for something we're lacking or to make up for something we've got too much of. Madness runs the gamut from sweet, happy, peaceful la-la land to far beyond the scariest thing we can think of. All it takes is one more step or one more plug into your already overloaded sockets.

When life is seriously overwhelming, it's okay to check out if that's what's going to keep you alive. Sometimes diving into our deepest madness is the only reason or way to stay alive. If that's the case, try to find yourself a doctor, healer, or loving community of friends who will help you descend into your madness and return in one piece.

But wait! Before you dive into whatever frightening pit of demons and grasping devils awaits you, try *consciously* checking out first. It can help with the pain, whether it's physical or emotional. When I'm in pain, I have a place I try to visualize. It's a little island off the coast of Maine in the northeast United States. It's not much of an island; you can see from one end of it to the other. But there's a dock where seals come to play. There are a few trees where some friendly raccoons live. And all the animals I've ever lived with are there. And by the time I visualize all of that, the pain is pretty much gone—or I'm gone from it. It's a form of conscious madness called visualization.

WHAT IF YOU'VE REALLY GOT IT ALL TOGETHER? Maybe there's a version of someone else's madness that would make your life better to live. Try to choose a madness that makes you feel better and that best lines up with your life's dream.

RECOMMENDED: *Girl, Interrupted* (the movie and the book). The films *The Fisher King*, and *King of Hearts*. Anything Tori Amos. For wonderfully intricate and magically transforming tales of diving into madness, try the Tales from the Flat Earth series by Tanith Lee. *The Little Endless Storybook* written and illustrated by Jill Thompson is a warm tale about safeguarding madness.

69. GO ON A SERIAL SUICIDE SPREE.

   YG

KEYWORDS: spirit, clean slate, empowering

Laugh at your own funeral, dance on your own grave, and then skip off to live a whole new life. Don't kill yourself! Kill off the *part* of you that badly needs to die.

Of course you are simply you, but you are also many versions of you that you create to deal with the world: You are the you that you are with your friends. You are the you that you are with a bully.

You are the you that you are with your parents, your boss and your lover(s).

Some of the you's that you've created are like Frankenstein's monster. You tried, but you goofed. Other you's might be really creepy. They embody selfish, mean, or self-destructive parts of you, rather than the loving parts of who you are. Maybe you're feeling ashamed or guilty about that particular you. Well, kill that you off! It's as easy as one-two-three!

ONE: Make a list of the qualities that describe who that unwanted part of you is, what that part of you does, and the values that part of you hangs on to. Give that part of you a name.

TWO: Figure out the sweetest way it could die.

THREE: Kill it the way it's always wanted to die.

DEBUG MODE: Having trouble finding different parts of yourself? Use #42, Act your age or any other, and #43, Act your gender or any other.

70. GET A MAKEOVER.

KEYWORDS: delight, clean slate, comfort

People have been marking and changing their bodies for thousands of years and for almost as many reasons. It's no big deal. Still, when you cross the line into what the culture considers body modifications inappropriate to who and what they expect you to be, you brand yourself an outsider.

Regardless, there are good reasons to mark or change your body, both temporarily and permanently. Aside from reasons of health or strength, I've changed or marked my body for all of the following:

To remember	To blend in better	To repel
To remind	To proclaim	To inspire
To honor	To mark as property	To belong
To welcome	To reveal	To enjoy
To amuse	To beautify	To shock
To sanctify	To encourage	For the sex
To show respect	To attract	For the pain

If you're changing your body more radically than trimming your hair or toning up your muscles, here are some questions you're going to want to have good answers for:

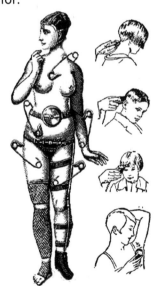

Why do you want to change or mark yourself?

How permanent would you like the mark or change to be?

From what emotional space are you making your decision to mark or change your body?

How much pain are you willing to endure?

How will your body modification affect your ability to navigate different cultures?

71. GEEK OUT.

KEYWORDS: real life, empowering, comfort

 Are you obsessed with computers, science, comic books, gaming, spaceships, weird science, or revolution? Are you more comfortable with a keyboard than you are with face-to-face conversation? Do you speak Klingon better than you do English? Great! With that point of view, you're going to discover new ways to create art, to play a better game, and to subvert the dominant paradigm, or just plain make yourself feel better geeking out, and that's the whole geeking point, isn't it?

RECOMMENDED: Check out www.geekculture.com. Say hey to Snaggy and Nitrozac for me.

Important reminder to all readers...

No single alternative to killing yourself will ever be enough for a jumbo-sized soul like you! Make sure you have another alternative stashed in your trunk, ready to pull out when you need it.

72. GIVE UP NOUNS FOR A DAY.

   G

KEYWORDS: mind game, spirit, delight

Nothing remains in the same state or place. That's not a chair you're sitting on, it's chairing. Right now, that collection of molecules in motion is continuously forming itself into a chair, over and over again. After a while, some of those molecules get tired of being part of a chair, and they drop off to become something else. That's called decay. Recovering addicts and alco-

holics get this when they say, "this too shall pass." Spend a day without using any nouns and write down your observations.

73. MAKE A NAME FOR YOURSELF IN THE WORLD.

   G

KEYWORDS: safety, empowering, thrill ride

You don't have to use or put up with a name for yourself that doesn't make you feel good. You get to name yourself. If a name works for you someplace in the world but not in other places, you get to use multiple names. Outlaws have been doing that for a long time. Like cats, we change the names we respond to. We change names to shift who we are, or to signal the nature of our desire, or to signal how we want to exercise power within a given sphere. Whatever it is you call yourself, it had better be as flexible as you'd like yourself to be.

EXERCISE: Make a list of all the names you go by and all the names that other people call you. Use #38, Cast a spell, to cast out the names you no longer want to use and another spell to protect the names you want to be known by. Keep one name for yourself only.

74. FRAME YOUR OWN DEBATE.

   G

KEYWORDS: purpose, mischief, mind game

Is someone calling you fag, dyke, fatso, nigger, queer, whore, spick, geek, chink, nerd, beaner, kike, or freak? Any combination of these?

These words will bother you a whole lot less when you stop buying into the system that allows this oppression as an option.

If some system or other is making it difficult for you to be accepted, much less celebrated, for who and what you are, then opt out. Find the courage to call out its blind spots and refuse to acknowledge its narrow, oppressive framework.

When someone calls you a name, and you say, "No, I'm not that!" you keep the name in place. At best, your denial only identifies you as not being the name, rather than as *being* the wonderful something else that you are.

I know that terms like fag, dyke, guy in a dress, man and woman can't come close to properly defining who and what I am. So, I've been working at reframing the system of gender that insists on these classifications. Reframing is a lot like redefining. It's about positioning yourself in a way that does not play into the hands of a culture that wants to diminish you. When I'm called names now, it's as though they come at me in slow motion, giving me time to easily dodge them, like Neo or Trinity in *The Matrix* trilogy. I'm not claiming I can do this every time, but I'm getting better and better at it.

ADVANCED MODE: Once you've reframed a debate, get your new frame more widely agreed upon in order to shift the paradigm of a group or your home, school, business, or country. See #95, Play to a broader audience, and #92, Choose your battles wisely.

RECOMMENDED: For more on the mechanics of framing a debate and how it applies to national politics, read *Don't Think of an Elephant* by George Lakoff. And do watch *The Matrix* trilogy a couple of times. It's a great reframing of American bully culture.

75. USE ANOTHER WORD FOR HELLO.

   G

KEYWORDS: delight, spirit, real world

Do you know what "hello" means? I don't. And I find it a little scary that we're a culture of people who greet each other with a word that no one understands. Try greeting people differently. Say what you mean when you see someone. If you don't know someone, you can always wish them a good morning, good afternoon, or good evening. *Namaste* (NAH-mah-stay) is a good word to use. Roughly, it means, "I see that you and I share a common spirit and that pleases me." Spend a day greeting people in some way that genuinely expresses your happiness in seeing them. See if that makes a difference in your mood.

76. LEARN ANOTHER LANGUAGE OF LOVE.

   **YG/ASS**

KEYWORDS: spirit, delight, safety

Relationships have a lot to do with the coevolution of a language, or languages, that make it safe to say what we mean, and trust that we're being heard. If you want to understand your lover or lovers, and you want them to understand you, you'll need to share several languages so that you may communicate verbally, physically, emotionally, and spiritually about power, identity, and desire. A safe language would mean that you and your lover have a way to tell each other what you want, what you don't want, what you're willing to try, and what your limits are—whether it's sex you're talking about, or living arrangements, or finances, or anything else. Both of you have the right to say yes, no, stop, and slow down. Here are some other basic words and phrases for you and your lover(s) to know and agree on:

Hello.	I've enjoyed this time with you.
I'm not going to hurt you.	I do not want to see you again.
Am I interrupting?	Please.
May I join you?	Thank you.
Where are your boundaries?	Good-bye.
Here are my boundaries.	and my favorite . . .
What pleases you?	Thank you, Sir. May I have
This is what pleases me.	another?

IMPORTANT: Sometimes, despite your charm, intelligence, and great good looks, there will be people you're attracted to who are not attracted to you. The reason he, she or they said no may have very little to do with you. Let go and move on. Someone just as neat or better is out there looking for you. See #46, Find the love of your life.

77. FLIRT WITH DEATH.

   YG/ASS

KEYWORDS: thrill ride, spirit, if you must

This is not a smart thing to do. But we all do it once. We'll stick a screwdriver into an electrical socket or smoke in bed. Or we'll stand closer and closer to the railroad tracks each time a train is coming. Some people still have unprotected sex. Some people try crack cocaine. Some people take painkillers before they go to an S/M play party. Have you ever done anything like that? Did you like it? Wanna do it again? It's only barely an alternative to killing yourself. Try doing it via a film or video game first, please. But if you must flirt with Death, I expect you to remember your manners and be a perfect lady or gentleman, regardless of your gender.

FLIRTING DO'S AND DON'TS:

Study Death. Every girl likes to know her beau has made an effort to get to know her better.

Smile! No one—not even Death—likes to hang out with a grumpy poo-poo head! Put a smile on your face using the emotional scale and instructions in the Hello, Cruel Quick-Start Guide. Remember, the best time to flirt with Death is when *you're* feeling best about your life!

Study Birth. It's also part of Death's job, and she'll be delighted that you're taking an interest in her work.

Don't push Death! If Death isn't flirting back, take the hint and stop it. Go flirt with Life instead.

There are more tips on flirting with Death in these films: *Boys Don't Cry, Secretary, All That Jazz, Crash* (Cronenberg), *Fight Club*, and *High Art*. And read anything at all by Heather Lewis, because this alternative is lovingly dedicated to her memory.

78. MAKE IT BLEED.

   YG-50

KEYWORDS: relief, if you must

For thousands of years and across many cultures, outcasts, outlaws, freaks, and holy people have cut themselves for a variety of harmless reasons they've felt to be important. I am a cutter and a masochist. I don't cut myself because I hate myself or any particular part of my body, but I started out that way.

Cutting yourself is a valid alternative to killing yourself if you feel it is your least self-harming option, but it can quickly spiral out of control. If you're cutting—or if you're thinking about it—it doesn't make you a bad person. But what's your reason for cutting? To heal? To feel? To punish? There are other, safer ways to do all those things. Please do not start cutting yourself if you can help it.

I cut because when I see my blood, it reminds me that I'm alive. Or I cut myself to mark the deaths of loved ones. I cut to make my anguish, grief, or rage leave my body through my blood. Or I cut to proclaim myself a warrior.

So bleed, if that's what it takes to keep you alive another day. If you're going to cut yourself, please try to cut with conscious self-love, never with self-loathing. If you're doing that, or you're cutting yourself out of anger or disgust, or you feel that it's getting out of control, see a doctor because you're in over your head and you need help.

79. TAKE DRUGS. NO, REALLY. TAKE DRUGS.

   YG

KEYWORDS: if you must

Drugging yourself is a valid alternative to killing yourself, but taking drugs without medical or spiritual supervision can easily put you in the position of doing dumb and sometimes harmful things to yourself and to others. If you're doing drugs—or if you're thinking about doing drugs—it doesn't make you a bad person. Doing illegal drugs does make you a criminal, and it can land you in jail. However dumb that is, it's something you want to keep in mind.

There is a drug out there that will make you feel better. That's both the good news and the bad news. Any debate about drugs comes down to this formula: if I put X into my body, I will feel Y. Well, everything you put into your body makes you feel this way or that. If you want to feel better and you find yourself unable to answer any of the following questions about something you want to put into your body, try putting something more self-loving into your body instead:

What is it about your life that taking a drug would make better? I'm not saying don't take drugs. I'm just saying that if you don't answer this question, you'll never have a good reason to judge if your drug of choice is working or not. I'll tell you this much: drugs will not cure your race, age, class, gender, sexuality, popularity, or tax problems.

What is the least harmful substance you can take into your body to make yourself feel better? Please, don't take Vicodin if nicotine will do the trick. And don't take either of those without first trying a nice calming cup of herbal tea. Try to make do with the least harmful drug you can come up with for whatever it is that's ailing you. How can you tell if a drug is harmful? Some drugs will work the first time, the second time, the third time, and maybe even more times after that. Then you'll start to need a larger dose to get the same feeling. If that happens, stop taking that drug. It is not a good drug for you, no matter how good it feels or how much it hurts to stop taking it.

How long do you keep on taking it? Remember, no single alternative to killing yourself is going to work all the time. What alarm are you setting yourself to let you know it's time to switch to another way to keep yourself alive?

How do you stop? Before you start, talk with people who've stopped. Read their stories. Are you prepared to do the kinds of things they've done to stop?

Look, if you are so scared or so hurting or so anything that you just want to get away from it all and none of the other alternatives in this book seem to be working for you, please go see a qualified psychiatrist, nutritionist, or health practitioner. There may be something safe you can take that will make you feel better, and it doesn't cost a million dollars or your soul. But if you tried that and it still didn't work, I'd be a damned mean fool to tell you that killing yourself is better than taking drugs. But here are some things you might want to keep in mind before you take stronger drugs:

♦ There's no guarantee you'll be able to stop. Ever.
♦ Most drugs are illegal to consume or sell. Are you prepared to face the consequences if you are caught?
♦ Drugs of any kind will likely make you less capable of connecting and communicating well with anyone.
♦ Taking any kind of drug, including steroids, will make it difficult for you to work your body well in relationship to your surroundings.
♦ Hallucinogens are rarely fun by yourself. They're much cooler with a spiritually oriented, experienced guide. Why? If you're taking any kind of hallucinogen, boiling hot water might look to you like a cool, refreshing, babbling brook— or the fiery depths of Hell itself. You're never really sure.

♦ While you're on drugs, including caffeine and sugar, you can act pretty stupid. With every drug you take, it's likely that you won't know that you're not communicating or acting well in the world.

♦ Every single drug you might want to take to feel better comes with some degree of physical addiction. That means your body will constantly be telling you it wants and needs more, and it'll make you sick to some degree if you don't get it.

♦ Please don't share needles. You could end up with the latest plague and a whole other set of problems to deal with on top of the problems you're taking the drugs to avoid dealing with in the first place. Find yourself a needle exchange program.

♦ And what about the cost of drugs? They get very expensive. You might indeed resort to stealing from people in order to pay for them. Is that something you're prepared to do?

Good luck.

80. GET CLEAN OR SOBER, STAY DIRTY OR DRUNK.

KEYWORDS: if you must

> WARNING: Reading this may act as a trigger if you are working on a rigorous program of recovery. And no one in their first year of recovery should try it. I mean it. Get clean and sober. Do it. Me, I'm twenty-five years sober, and for the last fifteen years I haven't been very clean. It doesn't work for everyone.

PLEASE DON'T FUCK WITH THIS ONE IF YOU CAN HELP IT.

I'm no longer a member of Alcoholics Anonymous, though I still go to meetings from time to time. When it comes to drugs, if they're there, I'll usually do some. If they're not, I won't. That's how I seem to be wired. Not all AA members embrace me as sober, and they probably wouldn't embrace a stoned sober you. Just like Narcotics Anonymous members probably wouldn't embrace a drunk but clean you. But it's worth going to a meeting even if you aren't gold-star clean and sober.

MESSAGE FOR SPONSORS: Please help your outlaw sponsee stay sober, whether or not he, she, or ze is clean. Please help your sponsee stay clean whether or not he, she, or ze is sober. I'm asking you to trust your sponsee to handle it as long as he, she, or ze follows *your* program.

POSTMODERN MODE: Develop a workable meeting for pomoholics who are trying to do it in the gray zone. But please . . . do not quit your twelve-step day job until you know the new one works.

81. STARVE YOURSELF.

   G

KEYWORDS: if you must

Starving yourself is a valid alternative to killing yourself, but only just barely. If you're starving yourself either by not eating or by throwing up what you eat—or if you're thinking about doing that—it doesn't make you a bad person, but you do need medical help. Use another alternative in this book to stay alive while you stop doing this one. This alternative is the most deadly in the book.

How bad is it? Anorexia can kill you, and in most cases it does. If it doesn't kill you, it can cause permanent damage to any number of organs. The organ most likely to get screwed up is your heart.

And what do you get out of starving yourself? Maybe some time of being corpse thin. Disappear into thin air thin. But you can never enjoy it, because you're never thin *enough*. Ever. But you keep on trying. So, you get really bad-looking thin. Sunken eyes, brittle bones, maybe your hair's falling out, but you're too tired to notice or care and your body is covered with something that isn't quite feathers. Then you die, neither peacefully nor painlessly. It's really hard to find anything that's less self-loving than starving yourself.

That said, I've been an active anoretic for the past forty years. My anorexia is periodic, meaning it comes and it goes. I've been hospitalized for anemia, which is what they called it when boys were anoretic in the 1960s. Not eating is something I can do that isn't screaming or lashing out at someone. My anorexia has kept me alive on several occasions when I just wanted to die. It seems I can handle not eating like some people can handle alcohol. You may or may not be that kind of anoretic. Either way, there is no real payoff except the few more days it gives you to find some other reason to stay alive.

Sometimes, to avoid completely starving myself, I stop eating overly processed foods, sugar, and white flour. They aren't good for you anyway. But if cutting back on sweets or fats or carbohydrates or processed foods doesn't work, Weight Watchers always does. While I'm high on my anorexia, it's the hunger itself that triggers me further. They taught me how to eat balanced, satisfying meals so that I can maintain a healthy weight without ever being hungry, and it's sort of fun being one of the few freaky people in one of those meetings.

Remember, anorexia is gender free. Boys and men starve themselves, too. Even heterosexual boys and men. It doesn't mean they're gay or transsexual or anything but anoretic.

CYBER TIP: There are caring, affirmative online communities of people with eating disorders. Some of them are all about getting over your eating disorder. Some of them are about supporting you in your decision to live as long as you can as an active anoretic or bulimic.

RECOMMENDED: There are a lot of good memoirs and personal

narratives. *Wasted* by Marya Hornbacher and the novel *Hungerpoint* by Jillian Medoff are both smart, scary, kind, and funny. See also the WGBH Nova documentary *Dying to Be Thin*.

82. PLAY MUSICAL ADDICTIONS.

   G

KEYWORDS: if you must, thrill ride

What's an addiction? Anything you do upon which you're physically or mentally dependent. If you're addicted to something, it's difficult to stop without adverse effects.

DELICIOUS

I've got an addictive personality, which to me means that at any given moment, one or another addiction is more or less active. It's like that arcade game, Whack-a-Mole, where you try to hit moles that pop up and down. It finally dawned on me that I was unconsciously moving from one addiction to another and that I could somehow harness this little ride and consciously shift addictions. This is not the very best way to handle things, but it does work in a pinch. Try to move toward less and less self-harming addictions if you possibly can.

83. PLEAD INSANITY.

   YG/ASS

KEYWORDS: safety, delight, mischief

Instead of judging yourself guilty as much as you do, be the judge and find yourself *not* guilty by reason of insanity. I learned that from a very sweet gay Catholic priest. The Dalai Lama says something along the same lines. When I saw him speak in New York City, someone asked him what to do when you've done something really bad or you've made a big mistake. "Forgive yourself," he said, "and try to do better next time."

> IMPORTANT: If you've never felt guilty about anything, ever, please tell that to a doctor or counselor or therapist. It's like having no feeling in your fingertips and resting them on a hot stove. Everyone has some guilt. You're just not feeling it, and it's burning the hell out of you even if you don't know it.

84. DEFY PROPHECY.

    G

KEYWORDS: clean slate, purpose, relief

Many people are awfully fond of predicting what will happen to other, especially younger, people. Most of their prophecies don't amount to very much at all. But every once in a while, someone else's less-than-pleasant prediction of our futures will match up exactly with our low self-esteem or self-doubts, and we'll begin to make someone else's prophecy come true.

So, defy prophecy. Write down everything you can remember that anyone predicted about what you would be, what you would do, or what you would wind up with (or without) by the time you were the age you are right now. Put a star by any of the predictions that came true. Put an X by any that didn't. And by those for which it's too early to tell, put a question mark. Next to each, write down the name of the person who said it. Which are your truest prophets? Which are false?

At the time the predictions were made, which did you think would come true? Were any of these predictions kind? Were any of them unrealistic given who you were at the time? Now, of the predictions that may still come true, put a heart next to the ones that make you feel better about yourself. Write *false* in big letters through the predictions that make you feel worse about yourself. Write realistic, fun prophecies to replace the false ones.

85. THROW AWAY MORALS.

   YG/ASS

KEYWORDS: self-esteem, relief, mischief

Moral codes are the sociological equivalent of training wheels. Theoretically, all moral restrictions could be lifted once people are traversing the world more or less kindly. People would just be nice to each other. Moral codes are useful only when we have descended to needing them. The Ten Commandments or the

Beatitudes come in handy when we have to make an important decision, or when we're under a great deal of pressure, or when we're thinking about killing ourselves or someone else. We don't have to think too hard, we just remember, "Thou shalt not kill."

The problem with most moral codes today is that they don't have much to do with what's actually good for people. They exist primarily to direct us into predictable and controlled behaviors. People who write moral codes into law don't trust you. They think you and I have to be kept strictly in line. That's called a theocracy, and you don't have to stand for it. It's healthier for your soul to live outside and above a degraded moral code than within and beneath one.

Prior to throwing away morals altogether, put together and live by your own moral code—one that works and allows you to live a kind and generous life. Make a list of all the moral rules you were raised with. Throw away the ones that don't work for you, and keep the ones that do. Once you're good at living within the boundaries of your own moral code, then you can throw it away and simply get on with living a kind and generous life.

RECOMMENDED: *1984* by George Orwell, *The Handmaid's Tale* by Margaret Atwood, and any version you like of the *Tao Te Ching*.

86. IGNORE THE GOLDEN RULE.

   G

KEYWORDS: empowering, spirit

My grrlfriend reminded me that there's only one rule to follow in this book, so the Golden Rule had to go. Besides, everyone *else* ignores the Golden Rule. Why should *you* be the only poor slob who actually obeys it?

One less rule to think about following means more time to look at *me!*

Let's take this thing apart. The Golden Rule is an ethical command, which makes it somewhat more significant than mere morals, which can fluctuate with cultures and subcultures. The Golden Rule is supposed to work for anyone. Do unto others as I would have them do unto me, but which me? And frankly, I really enjoy having things done unto me that not too many people would enjoy having done unto them. How about you? Better to ignore the Golden Rule. If you'd like to follow the *spirit* of the Golden Rule, just get into the habit of treating people better than they think they deserve to be treated. That ought to make everyone feel just great.

87. QUOTE SCRIPTURE FOR YOUR OWN PURPOSES.

KEYWORDS: mischief, empowering

You can't just dismiss an entire movement or religion simply because part of it is a little batty when it comes to people like you. Part of *you* is a little batty when it comes to someone *else*. Yes, it can be more than a little intimidating to find yourself and people like you being railed against in some religious text. If some harmless joy of yours is forbidden or sneered at in some scripture, you can safely assume that the scripture wasn't written for people like you, and you are under no obligation to subscribe to it. Instead, go find

There is neither Jew nor Greek. There is neither bond nor free. There is neither male nor female. For ye are all one in Christ Jesus.

3rd Galatians, v. 28

yourself some scripture that you *do* agree with, and quote it for your own purposes. Look at the quote in this illustration. The Bible says there's no such thing as male or female. I *love* that. You can find something like that for yourself.

DO-IT-YOURSELF SCRIPTURE FINDING: Study scripture and write down all the quotes that support who and what you are in the world, and what you believe in. Use them to make zines, stickers, and posters to your heart's delight.

ADVANCED MODE: Join a scripture discussion group of a religion that disapproves of something you do in your life. Try to be as nice and respectful as you can, please.

ADVANCED MODE, ON THE OTHER HAND: If, on the other hand, it's simply a huge relief to part with a religion's scriptures and it's painful to review them, then go to #85, Throw away morals, and #48, Find your tribe.

RECOMMENDED: *Sensuous Spirituality* and *Omnigender* both by dear, wise, handsome Virginia Ramey Mollenkott and *The Women's Encyclopedia of Myths and Secrets* by Barbara Walker.

88. WRITE YOUR OWN CODE OF HONOR.

KEYWORDS: empowering, real life, purpose

There's a lot to be said for a thief's notions of honor, the pirates' code, and even the rules and regulations of old-school sadomasochists. But no one else's code of honor will work for you 100 percent. You're just going to have to come up with your own.

Codes of honor are simply guidelines we develop or subscribe to in order to remind ourselves to do deeds we can be proud of, and to avoid doing deeds we're ashamed of. Why? Doing things we're proud of makes us feel worthwhile, noble, and good. Doing things we're ashamed of makes us feel depressed and suicidal. So it becomes important to decide whose definition of shame we rely upon as a yardstick. You do not have to obey any code of honor that asks you to kill yourself for any reason.

Patch together a code of honor for yourself from codes that already exist. Study honorable people and deeds of honor. Look for the honor in everyone you meet. Most outlaw subcultures develop their own codes of honor. Try Googling "code of honor" and/or "honor code," along with the name of the outlaw culture you most resonate with. Carry your code of honor around with you and refer to it from time to time, making changes and adjustments as you need to.

89. SHATTER SOME FAMILY VALUES.

   G

KEYWORDS: spirit, empowering, mischief

Sex and gender outlaws are often accused of attacking traditional American family values. Look . . . *Don't kill anyone* is a value. *Don't be a homo* is not a value. Beyond making a few privileged people feel like they've been chosen by God, it makes no positive contribution to society whatsoever.

The unwritten, oft hinted at "family

values" that are used to beat up freaks are bogus. They've got nothing to do with family, and you should feel free to shatter them at will.

Here are some alternative outlaw values. The next time you're faced with an overwhelming problem, try this: 1. Pick out one or two values from this list that would most quickly resolve the issue. 2. Pick out the identity from Alternatives #42 and #43 that you could best use to implement that value. 3. Take on that identity and implement your value.

Home/Paradox	Integrity	Deconstruction
Transformation	Anarchy	Dreams
Service	Seasons	The dark side
Passion	Trust	Unconditional love
Security	Patience	Freedom
Faith	Death	Mindful Reconstruction/
Sex	Art	Home
Control	Humor	

90. BELIEVE IN YOUR OWN LAUGHTER.

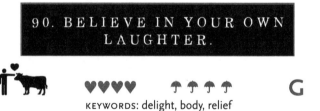

KEYWORDS: delight, body, relief

Laughter alone can make you feel better. Your body knows the truth of your laughter and responds with a release of endorphins that makes you feel great. Even if you are über-grouch or über-Goth, you have smiled and laughed enough times during this lifetime for your body to know this: when you smile or laugh, something is funny or pleasing, and that feels good. Smile, right now. Go ahead. When I make myself smile when nothing is particularly funny or pleasing, I can feel the echo in my body of fun and pleasure. If this resonates at all for you, try any number of books on laughter therapy, or check out www.teehee.com.

What kinds of things make you laugh? Keep a small notebook with you and write them down. Put a star next to the ones that aren't at anyone else's expense. Put two stars next to the ones that aren't at your expense either. Do a lot more of the two-star things than the one-star things. Do a lot more of the one-star things than the no-star things. That'll brighten up yer day.

91. BELIEVE IN YOUR OWN PARADOX.

    G

KEYWORDS: spirit, delight, mind game

What is it that puzzles you most? Is there something going on in your life or around you that doesn't quite make sense? Confusion is how you know you're close to something big. Contradiction is how you know you've hit the nail on the head. Some of the most loving people I know are intense sadists. The most

218 • Hello, Cruel World

handsome man in my life has a vagina. I am neither a man nor a woman, and I am both. Do you have that kind of stuff going on in your life?

Have you ever followed your curiosity to two different parts of your life, each of which makes sense on its own, but together, cancel one another out? Coming to terms with your own paradox is a jim-dandy way to go on living.

STEP ONE: Experience paradox. Pick a question that interests you from the following list. Each one will lead you to at least one pair of rational opposite answers or opposite points of view, both of which are true. Consider that pair of concepts until you can hold them in your mind as true, both at the same time.

> *Are cats and dogs children of God?*
>
> *Why are so many scary people, places, and things so tempting?*
>
> *Why do good people do mean things?*
>
> *Can someone be a bad person and still lead a good life?*
>
> *Why is terrorism so prevalent in the world?*
>
> *Is unconditional love possible?*
>
> *Can someone be completely passionate and completely reasonable at the same time?*
>
> *What can account for the fact that the sixty-four hexagrams of the* I Ching *bear striking similarities to the structure of the DNA that's inside every single living thing?*

*True or false: if you could stand on the edge of a
black hole and look back over your shoulder,
you'd see all of time behind you.*

*Are heterosexual sex and homosexual sex both
natural?*

*Why is it, do you suppose, that in a henhouse where
there's no rooster, one of the chickens will begin
crowing at dawn?*

Are there friendly demons and nasty-tempered fairies?

Can justice be both blind and fair?

*Can a person be popular and a freak at the same
time?*

Is time invariably linear?

*Can people be patriots and disagree with or criticize
their government?*

*Can a person be attracted to both men and women
and people who are neither?*

*Can sex be really vulgar and really beautiful at the
same time?*

*Are you both relieved and disappointed that we've
come to the end of these questions?*

STEP TWO: Experience your own paradox. Work with any of the
following questions and concepts, each of which should lead you
to some paradox about yourself. Consider that paradox until you
can hold it in your mind as neither a good thing nor a bad thing
about yourself.

Is there anything in your life that both gives you a great deal of joy and gets you in the most trouble?

Do you find yourself having to be two nearly opposite kinds of people in different situations or with different people?

Is there something about yourself that if you told people about it, it would totally change their opinion about who and what you are?

When was the last time you laughed and cried at the same time?

Who is it that you never want to see again but wish you could give a hug?

Why do some people think you're really bad, even though you're not much of a mean person?

STEP THREE: Put your paradoxes into words. Paradoxes can be frustrating to the degree that we are unable to communicate them to other people. Fill in the blanks about yourself as many times as you care to:

I am being completely honest when I say that I am _____.

Am I _____ or _____?

I am both _____ and _____ and neither.

I simultaneously love and hate _____.

The last time I killed a part of myself, _____.

The next time I kill a part of myself, _____.

I'm alive because _____.

ARTSY MODE: Express your paradox in the art form of your choice.

92. CHOOSE YOUR BATTLES WISELY.

   YG/ASS

KEYWORDS: safety, empowering, purpose

As peaceful and nonviolent as you'd like yourself to be, your life will undoubtedly include fighting. You're battling the people who think you're too fat or too poor or too girly or too butch, or that think you're a terrorist or a traitor. You're battling the people who never give you a break and always want more than you can possibly give. You're battling injustice

At what times in your life are you one of these marchers? And at what times in your life are you the one they're marching against?

as best as you know how. Or, you're battling the traffic on the way home from school or work. We all fight, and if you're reading this book, chances are you're battle weary. You can only take on so much at any given time. The question becomes, how do you choose your points of engagement?

Try this: List the battles you're currently waging and prioritize them. Which can be won the soonest and with the least effort? Pick the ones you know you can win, and go out there and win them. Pick the hard ones that are most important to you, and battle for them too, even if all odds are against you.

And while all these battles are going on in your life, continually train yourself as a warrior. When possible, learn patiently from an inspiring teacher. Read *The Art of War* by Sun Tzu. You can download it for free. Print a copy and carry it around with you. You want to be a leader? You will be.

RECOMMENDED: *A Book of Five Rings* by Miyamoto Musashi, the films *Patton* and *Lawrence of Arabia*, the TV series *Firefly*, and any of several productions of *Henry V* by William Shakespeare.

93. BRING ON GOLIATH.

   YG/ASS

KEYWORDS: safety, purpose, clean slate

David was a shepherd who wrote racy poetry. Goliath was a monstrously strong, highly experienced warrior sent by the Philistine commanders to challenge the Israelis over some part of the Middle East. Every day Goliath would roar his humiliating challenge to the Israelites: "Where is there among you a champion who will fight me on behalf of all of Israel?" Of course, no one dared answer. For six days, the commanders of the Israeli army faced humiliation as Goliath was daily met by silence, broken only by his haughty laughter. But, on the seventh day, just as Goliath began to laugh and turn

 away, dreamy hippie David stepped out in front of Goliath and said, "I'll take your challenge, Mister!"

While Goliath was overcome by laughter, David calmly twirled his sling and fired a rock into his head.

Boom! Goliath was toppled, and David, the poet and sheep lover, went on to become the King of Israel. Talk about postmodern identity switching. What have you learned from all this?

You can do what David did. You've got a weapon, too: the perspective of an outsider, which gives you the ability to see situations from multiple points of view. Before you hurl the rock, first try turning your Goliath into an ally. Failing that, what would it take to surprise, seduce, charm, or shock *your* Goliath right between the eyes?

94. SPEAK WITH YOUR EARS.

KEYWORDS: empowering spirit purpose

The chakras are energy centers located in the body. Eastern healers, philosophers, and holy people have known them for thousands of years. You may have heard of the Third Eye, located on your forehead, right between your eyes. But there's also the Third Ear. It's an energy center located in your  throat. It's called "the voice that listens." You can hear a voice that listens in folks like Terry Gross, Jon Stewart, Oprah Winfrey, Bill Clinton, Ted Koppel, and dear Phil Donahue. Go, grasshopper, and practice speaking with the voice that listens.

95. PLAY TO A BROADER AUDIENCE.

KEYWORDS: purpose, real life, safety

Have you got a message to get out to the world? Get it out there. You can do it. Try the following:

1. First, practice getting your message across to people who already agree with you. Do that for awhile, refining your message as you go.

2. Next, get your message out to people who *might* agree with you because they have interests similar to yours. Do that for awhile, refining as you go.

3. Then, practice getting your message across to people who *disagree* with you on most everything. Do that for awhile, again, refining as you go.

4. Now, compare the message you started with to the message you ended up with. Refine your message so that you can still call it your truth.

5. Repeat steps 1–4.

ART MODE: Do you want a larger audience for your art, but you don't want to sell out on your values? Apply the above five steps to the art form that best allows you to express yourself. Keep modifying your art so that more people are willing to experience it. You're stretching the acceptance level of your audience, and your audience is stretching your own level of articulation. Ride the resilient edge of resistance. Keep your art as true to yourself and your values as you can, and keep making your art more and more accessible to more and more people.

96. TAKE A VOW OF SILENCE.

KEYWORDS: comfort, real life

When you stop speaking, you can hear what the world really sounds like. You can use a vow of silence when it hurts too much to talk or whenever you just want to listen for a while. You can take a vow of silence when you've said what you feel is enough, and it's time for someone else's voice to be heard.

Do some research on silence. Find out why holy people, musicians, and artists take limited or permanent vows of silence. Apply what you find to your own life or art, and take a vow of silence for two days.

OPTIONAL NEXT STEP: Combine a vow of silence with #7, Trash your preference files and reboot. Reboot into #94, Speak with your ears. That should make for a fun reset.

ZEN MODE: Silly rabbit, Zen *is* silence.

RECOMMENDED: Anything by John Cage.

97. TAKE A WALK IN THE WOODS.

   G

KEYWORDS: body, comfort, spirit

Nature isn't something out there that grows food for us and supplies us with building materials, and fuel and water. We *are* Nature, and if we separate ourselves from what is natural for too long, some parts of ourselves may begin to feel like they're dying. Spending time with Nature is bound to make you feel natural.

Spend some time in a park, alone or with a friend. Go to the seashore and slide down some dunes. Hike a mountain trail, swim in a lake, or sunbathe on top of a levee. Go snowboarding. But even if all you do is open a window and breathe in the city air, *some* nature is better than none at all.

The time we spend plugged back into Nature reminds us that we are an integral part of a complex ecosystem and that all of us are trying to survive together under hellish circumstances. That's something you can forget if you live in a city or if the Nature you're spending your time in is too well manicured. Working in Nature gives us a body memory of what it's like to be connected to the earth. Resting in Nature reminds us how easy it is to feel healed and nourished, if only for a moment.

CONFINED-TO-BED MODE: Watch as many nature documentaries as you possibly can.

RAINY-DAY ACTIVITY: Walk in the rain without a hat, wig, umbrella, or raincoat.

ZEN MODE: Let the woods walk through you.

98. LEARN MODERATION IN ALL THINGS.

♥♥♥♥   ⬆ ⬆ ⬆ ⬆   G

KEYWORDS: real life, comfort, spirit

YOUR FACE HERE

Taking your own life is rarely a moderate thing to do, so this is pretty much a surefire alternative to killing yourself. But this is also the most difficult and frightening alternative in the book, because it brings you face-to-face with every monster and demon you've ever had to deal with: all the extremes of you. It is possible for you to make peace with all of that.

Begin your learning by doing *anything* more moderately. It's easier to initiate with a moderate action than it is to respond with a moderate action. As children, we learned that the way to respond to an extreme point of view is with an opposing and at least equally extreme point of view. That kind of reasoning says that when someone is shouting at you, you shout back as least as loud. Don't do that any more. Find another way to respond, a way that doesn't push back so hard against whatever it is that life is tossing at you.

ADVANCED MODE: Sooner or later in your travels through the horrors of learning moderation, you're going to realize that learning moderation in all things means learning to be moderate with moderation itself. It's Nature's way of saying thank you for being good.

RECOMMENDED: *Tao Te Ching* by Lao Tzu. I'm a big fan of the Stephen Mitchell translation. But visit your nearest woo-woo book resource and pick one that pings with you.

99. MAKE YOUR PEACE WITH DEATH.

   G

KEYWORDS: real life, comfort, spirit

No one alive knows what death is. No one alive can even prove the exact moment that death takes place. I truly don't mean any disrespect, but what the fuck is your rush?

You can live and die more or less at peace with your life and death, or you can live and die more or less in agony over your life and death. It's totally up to you, and it's not easy for anyone. Even if you're an accomplished peacemaker, it's an entirely different challenge to make peace with the unknown.

Try this: Write down all the reasons you

want to die. Each one of those reasons is bringing you closer to dying, so solving each one of those reasons is going to bring you closer to life. Solving each one of those issues while you're still alive is your life's to-do list. Do the easiest one first, and then the next, and then the next. As you solve all your reasons for dying, it gets easier to live. And this lets Death do her work in her own time, which could be a whole lot better time than the time you were considering for yourself.

100. TIDY YOUR CAMPSITE BEFORE YOU LEAVE.

   YG/ASS

KEYWORDS: clean slate, spirit, comfort

We can build up a lot of resentments and regrets moving from identity to identity, exploring desire after desire, and practicing with varying degrees of power. If we don't clean up after ourselves, we can leave quite a series of messes. The fair and honorable thing is to tidy up all your messes before you leave an identity, location, or station in life. But just like in the movies, we all sometimes have to pack up and leave town in a hurry, and we don't have time to clean up. Try your best to clean up before you leave anything, and don't even think about killing yourself until you're very, very good at this.

POST-FACTO MODE: Can you tidy your campsite in retrospect? Absolutely. Try the twelve-step style fearless personal inventory of all your deeds, then share that inventory with another person and make amends wherever possible. If that's too hard, say a sincere "I'm sorry."

101. TRY TO KEEP SOMEONE ELSE ALIVE.

KEYWORDS: real life, comfort, spirit

Dear Heart,

If you're considering this alternative to taking your own life, you've certainly been there and done plenty. Bless your heart, you're alive and kicking, and there's someone who could gain a great deal of strength and hope from hearing your story. With your heavily notated copy of *Hello, Cruel World* under your arm, you are ready to go out there and save some lives. Keep in mind that the best you can ever do is try. It's never your fault if you try to save someone's life and they kill themselves anyway. Whether or not you're successful, you'll release a great deal of good energy into the world. A lot of people all around you will feel better, whether or not they know that you had something to do with it. That's something you can enjoy.

There are plenty of suicide-prevention foundations that could use volunteers. You could get training as a counselor. Maybe there's a suicide hotline you could help staff. Maybe it's time to set one up in your area. Or maybe you just need to spend an evening talking with a friend. Enjoy life while you're doing that. I did, as best I could, while I was writing this book for you.

Thank you for the opportunity to contribute to your life span. I expect you'll make very good use of your extra years. And since I really don't like good-byes, I'll say, hello, cruel world. I believe it's a much better place for your being in it.

Love and respect always,

Kate

P.S.—if you were in this picture, who would you be? I'm just curious.

ABOUT THE AUTHOR

KATE BORNSTEIN is one of America's most original and thought-provoking authors and performance artists. The spunky insight of her wildly successful publications *Gender Outlaw: On Men, Women and the Rest of Us* and *My Gender Workbook: How to Become a Real Man, a Real Woman, the Real You, or Something Else Entirely* has revolutionized the way the world thinks about gender and identity. Assigned one gender at birth, but now living life as something else entirely, Kate identifies as neither a man nor a woman. Her books are taught in more than 120 colleges and universities around the world, and she has performed on college campuses, and in theaters and performance spaces, across the United States, as well as in Canada, the United Kingdom, Germany, and Austria. In 1996, she released *Nearly Roadkill: An Infobahn Erotic Thriller* with co-author Caitlin Sullivan. Kate currently lives with her partner, the sex pioneer, writer, and performance artist Barbara Carrellas, in New York City.

SARA QUIN is one part of the musical duo Tegan and Sara. She wears her pants too short, her shirts extra long, and travels with far too many bags to be even remotely organized. She always wanted to be a lawyer, but was easily persuaded into a life of rock and roll after high school. On rainy cold days, she likes to argue politics, human rights issues and cultivate her infatuation with Naomi Klein and bicycles.

For more on Kate and *Hello, Cruel World*, please visit www.hellocruelworld.net.

BONUS!
HELLO, CRUEL NOTE PAGES

(Use these pages to write down notes, secret messages, or love letters to yourself. Oh, go on!)